A Grower's Guide to
Annuals

Text by Margaret Hanks
Photographs by Lorna Rose

CRESCENT BOOKS
NEW YORK

CONTENTS

LEFT: Dwarf zinnias contrast with blue, pink and white petunias to make a glorious summer display of annuals.

ABOVE: The two-lipped shape of an old-fashioned snapdragon.

GROWING ANNUALS

No other plants can give your garden the splashes of color and seasonal interest that annuals do. Annuals can be planted in beds on their own, as borders to shrub plantings, as fillers of odd spaces and as accent plants in pots and hanging baskets

Annuals are plants that grow to full size, flower, seed and die within one year or one season. Generally, annuals are planted twice a year: in autumn to give a floral display through late winter and spring, and in spring to give garden color in summer and autumn.

There are annuals for almost every situation. Most grow best in sunny spots but there are some, such as cinerarias and primula, that prefer the shade. Do, however, be careful to plant at the correct time as some annuals are "short-day" plants and will not flower if the hours of daylight are too long. If you follow our planting guides and the directions on seed packets you should not have any trouble.

LEFT: The Victorian tradition of making patterns with low-growing annuals is here given a new look with blue violas, white sweet alyssum and the brilliant green of parsley.

ABOVE: Black-eyed Susan (Rudbeckia), a long-flowering summer daisy.

ROSES MAY BE THE QUEEN OF FLOWERS, but they look best with low-growing flowers to distract the eye from their thorny stems. Annuals, with their less competitive root systems, are perfect. Here the role is played by sunshine-bright portulacas, their color matching that of the roses.

SOIL PREPARATION

Good soil preparation will go a long way toward preventing problems with annuals. All annuals prefer well-drained soil, and so if you know that your soil is heavy and stays wet for long periods after rain, take steps to improve it before the planting season.

Heavy clay soils can be improved by adding lime or by digging in gypsum at the rate of about 6 oz per square yard. Digging in large quantities of well-decayed compost or manure will also help to improve aeration and drainage of heavy clays. In extreme cases you can even raise the level of the beds above the surrounding ground to ensure adequate drainage.

Very sandy soils or soils that dry out rapidly can also be improved by digging in copious quantities of well-rotted organic matter. The resulting humus will help to retain soil moisture and nutrients.

Dig in the compost or manure before planting: about four weeks before planting in warm weather and six to eight weeks in cool weather.

SEED OR SEEDLINGS?

You can grow your own annuals from seed or by buying seedlings. Starting from seed is cheaper and some annuals, such as sweet pea, nasturtium and sunflower, are best grown this way. They should be sown where they are to grow, and this is not difficult as the seed is large and easy to handle. Other plants, such as primula and poppy, have seed as fine as dust, which is not easy to sow well. If you mix a little fine sand with it you will find it easier to sow it evenly. Seed can be sown directly into the ground and thinned out later or started off in seed trays and planted out later.

Purchased seedlings have the advantage of putting you several weeks ahead and if you want a colorful display for a special occasion it is easier to gauge the time from planting to flowering. It is also possible to buy seedlings at the flowering stage for an almost instant effect. Or you can buy fully developed annuals that can be planted out into larger pots or straight into the garden. These are, of course, more expensive but they can give an immediate lift to a jaded garden or they can be used for temporary indoor decoration. These plants will continue blooming for several weeks if you are diligent about removing spent flowers.

SOWING SEED

Whether you sow your annuals from purchased or saved seed, always use a seed-starting mix unless you are sowing directly into the garden. You can use a commercial seed-starting mix or make your own from three parts coarse sand and one part peatmoss. Sow seed according to the packet directions and place pots or trays in a warm, sheltered spot.

Keep the mix just moist at all times, taking care that it is not too wet or the seedlings will rot. You may find it easier to water seed pots and trays from below to avoid the risk of dislodging seeds. Place your pot of seeds or tiny seedlings in a container holding water 1–2 in deep. Let the pot stand in the water long enough for the water to be drawn to the surface, and then remove the pot from the water. Allow the pot to drain and then replace it in its original location.

When growing seeds, it is very important to follow the specific directions: seed can fail when the mix is either too wet or too dry, or when the seed has been planted too deeply or at the wrong time of year. Once seedlings are large enough to handle, prick them out with a small fork or blade and place them in their permanent positions.

Most annuals grow best in temperate (warm to cool) climates, but some can be grown in cold or tropical areas and there are even a few for hot, dry areas. (See the

Flowering Chart on pages 106–7.) In very cold climates with a short growing season the range of annuals is rather restricted. Seeds of annuals that flower in late spring and summer need to be sown the previous autumn, inside or under glass, and grown on there until the danger of frosts is past. A climate map is on the inside back cover.

WATERING
All plants need regular watering to establish, but once they are established, reduce watering to a good soak once or twice a week. Some plants are adapted to poor or dry conditions and they do best if watered deeply only very occasionally. Check for the requirements of each plant.

FERTILIZING
When soil has been well prepared with compost or manure, plants usually perform quite well without additional fertilizer during the growing period. However, the addition of fertilizer should produce larger blooms on more vigorous plants. Some plants, such as nasturtiums, are best grown without extra fertilizer as this tends to send them into sappy leaf growth at the expense of flowers. These plants are adapted to grow in very poor conditions and perform poorly if given fertilizer or too much water.

You can start to fertilize your seedlings once they have become established. Some people prefer to use a liquid fertilizer about once every two weeks, others like to use a light dressing of granulated fertilizer placed alongside the plants. Whichever method you use, never apply fertilizer to bone dry soil. Water first, apply fertilizer, and then water again.

FLOWERING
Don't allow tiny plants to flower. As buds appear, pinch them out with your fingertips. If you allow annuals to flower when they are tiny they will never develop into good-sized plants and their life will be very short. It is also a good idea to pinch out the growing leaf tips to produce a bushier plant with more potential flowering stems.

To gain maximum flowering from your annuals you must be diligent about dead-heading. This means going over your plants about once a week and cutting off the spent flowers. If you don't remove the spent blooms, the plant will divert its resources into setting seed and stop producing a fresh crop of flowers.

SAVING SEED
If you want to save seed for the following year, allow the flowers to die naturally on the plant. Allow the seed-bearing organ (capsule or pod) that remains after the petals have dried and fallen to ripen and dry on the plant or the seed will not be viable.

Remember that flowers growing from the saved seed may not be identical to the previous crop. Many annuals today are what are known as F1 hybrids. To produce their seed, the breeder selects two specific strains of the plant. To get identical results a second time the same genetic crosses must take place naturally, and this is not likely. However, the display of flowers from saved seed is always interesting and you may find that some exciting and unexpected variations appear in your garden.

WHAT CAN GO WRONG?

Yellow leaves
● Plants may have been overwatered or may be too dry.
● Plants may need feeding—try feeding with a half strength solution of one of the soluble plant foods. If this is the problem you should see improvement within a week or two.

Curled or distorted leaves
● Look for aphids, small sticky insects clustering on the stems or leaves. Wash them off with the hose, spray with soapy water or use an insecticidal soap or pyrethrum.
● Check that herbicide has not been used nearby: a small amount of spray drift can cause this problem.
● Some virus diseases of plants manifest themselves this way. These are not common in annuals but there is no cure for virus disease in plants.

Black spots on leaves
● These may be fungal leaf spots. Avoid watering late in the day, try to avoid wetting leaves and spray plants with copper oxychloride if necessary.

Silvery trails in leaf tissue
● These may indicate leaf miner, especially on cinerarias or some daisies. It won't affect flowering but can be unsightly. However, control can only be achieved by spraying with a systemic insecticide such as dimethoate. It may be better to ignore the problem unless you are showing your garden in a competition.

Gray/white powder on leaf surfaces
● This could be powdery mildew, which is a problem on sweet peas. A spray with sulfur can halt the progress of the disease. Avoid watering late in the day.

Yellowish mottle on upper leaf, rusty brown spots on underside
● These probably are evidence of rust, a fungal disease that can be serious on snapdragons, calendulas and hollyhocks in particular. Remove the worst affected leaves, avoid watering late in the day and try not to wet the foliage. Spray plants with copper oxychloride, Zineb or Maneb.

Holes in leaves or leaf edges chewed
● This may be snail or slug damage. Search for snails and if you do not have dogs use one of the proprietary snail baits.
● Caterpillars, crickets and grasshoppers can also chew leaves. Try dusting your plants with rotenone over several consecutive nights so as to catch these culprits.

Seedlings cut off at ground level
● This is probably cutworm damage. These insects hide in the soil during the day and come out at night to feed. Dust the affected plants with rotenone or Sevin over several consecutive nights.

DESIGNING GARDENS FOR ANNUALS

Many home gardeners use annuals in drifts or blocks between other plants, but they can be used just as effectively on their own—and because of their short lives, they're the perfect flowers to use when you want to try out something a little bit different.

When separate beds are set aside for growing annuals the plants are usually set out in rows. If you have a large bed, try planting very tall flowers in a group in the center. You can then grade the sizes down until you reach the small edging plants. Or for a really informal garden, don't plant in rows at all—let the groups of plants intermingle and flow into one another to give a planting with a more natural appearance.

LEFT: *Cool colors always look refreshing in the glare of summer. Here catmint, white penstemons, lupins, blue salvias and pale rose mallow are set off by a range of gray-leafed perennials.*

ABOVE: *A delicately veined and shaded corn cockle flower.*

FORMAL GARDENS

Formal planting of annuals reached its peak in Victorian England where carpet bedding was all the rage, and recently there has been a revival of interest in this method of planting, especially on large estates and in municipal parks and gardens. Some home gardeners, too, are interested in creating a formal pattern in their gardens.

Formal bedding usually means a geometrical layout with strict rows of color creating shapes and patterns, often with a low border of box or what is known as exhibition border. A great deal of careful planning and maintenance must go into the creation of such a formal planting for it to be effective.

Planning for a very formal layout starts on paper. It is easiest to use graph paper so that you can simulate the scale of the planting and work out exactly where you want the colors to be. If you are doing true carpet bedding, you must choose plants that will all grow to the same height so as to create the tapestry or carpet effect. Many formal planting layouts tend to be restricted to just a few colors and species as the effect is in the pattern and textures.

COLD ZONE GARDENS

In cold areas annuals flower much later than in warm areas—often not until summer—but the floral display tends to last longer and the colors remain brighter without the bleaching effect of strong sun. In fact, cool zone gardeners often rely on massed bulb displays for their spring showing and use annuals to carry them through summer into autumn.

Some plants, such as larkspur and delphinium, which are annuals in warm areas can be treated as biennials (lasting two years) in cool areas. Columbine, which self-seeds readily, is often a feature of cool zone spring displays. All forms of viola, many of which are happier in cool areas, can be used for long-lasting displays and the colorful monkey flower grows to perfection.

A RIOT OF COLOR

Brilliant multi-colored effects can be achieved with annuals by planting drifts or blocks of single color plants, which can be just as striking as planting mixed colors at random. Many annuals, including verbena, petunia, viola, marigold, salvia, primula, lobelia, dianthus, cosmos, torenia and cockscomb, are available in single colors as well as mixtures.

A kaleidoscope of spring color is ready-made if you plant poor man's orchid alone or with other annuals. Mixed colors of ranunculus and anemone give a great display of color for the sunny garden and in shade or in cool areas mixed polyanthus create a multi-colored carpet of flowers. The rich blue, purple, magenta, cerise and pink of cinerarias also create great color in the shade.

For a small garden you need look no further than massed petunias or portulacas. Both will give vibrant color over a long period in summer as long as there is plenty of sun. For a stunning display of color in a large garden, plant amaranthus (Joseph's coat) as a tall (4 ft) background to bedding dahlias, cockscomb or zinnias. These annuals will give strong, almost tropical color to your summer garden.

WAX BEGONIAS in pink and white are used to make a bold demarcation between the lawn and shrubbery of this garden.

DISPLAY USING TWO COLORS

A more restrained effect can be achieved by creating a garden using only two colors. One popular combination these days is blue and yellow. You can achieve a lovely picture by planting blocks of plain yellow and plain blue violas. Simply alternate the colors or achieve more impact by planting in blocks. Small-flowered violas, which combine both colors, could be interspersed with other violas or used as a border. If you are planting a large area try tall royal blue cornflowers, paler blue love-in-a-mist and strong blue lobelias as an edging. The yellow/gold can be made up of marigolds, calendulas and wallflowers. All these blue and gold flowers will give you an attractive garden display through late winter and spring, and some of them, especially the violas and lobelias, will carry through into early summer.

Different effects can be created using two colors that are closely related in the spectrum. For a subdued effect mix pale blue with dark blue or purple flowers; for a warm result combine pink and red flowers; or try an old-fashioned combination of pink and mauve. A very different result will come by planting yellow and orange together to create a hot, vibrant effect.

Almost any color can be used with white for a lovely garden. For cool effects in summer try the green zinnia 'Envy' with white sweet alyssum, or clear yellow marigolds with white petunias.

BLUE FLOWERS HARMONIZE beautifully with just about any other color. Here a solid mass of floss flowers sets off the warm colors and more scattered flowers of the taller zinnias. (The camera sees the floss flowers as more mauve than the eye does.)

WHITE GARDENS

Beautiful gardens can also be created using only one color. They can be very elegant, with a simplicity and style often well suited to modern and formal gardens. A very small garden can also be effective planted in one color. The shapes and textures of the flowers and leaves will both play a part in creating a lovely effect, but make sure you place the tall plants at the back of the display so that they do not swamp the shorter ones.

White is a very popular choice for one-color gardens. The white flowers provide a sharp, cool contrast to the green foliage, and they are especially attractive in a shady or enclosed area.

For a spring display of white annuals, plant in the background tall, sweetly scented white column stock or chalk white candytuft—these are best in a sunny spot sheltered from strong wind. The foreground could be made up of ranunculus or anemone with a border of sweet alyssum. You should be able to buy these plants in single colors. White violas would be another choice for foreground planting and these will give a very long flowering if you are meticulous about removing the spent blooms from the plants every few days.

If your garden is fairly shady you will have to restrict your choice to annuals that flower reliably in shade. White primula and white cineraria are the best choice for the shaded garden and you can add white polyanthus here and there to light up a shaded corner. The primula will probably seed itself to provide plants for the following year and you may be able to carry over the polyanthus to flower again the next year.

In the summer garden white flowers create a cool look by day and can be an outstanding feature of the garden at night, giving added decorative effect when you are entertaining outdoors. Choice is more limited than in spring as fewer annuals are available in single colors and those available in white all need to be grown in the sun. For best results they should receive at least eight hours of full sun each day. Probably the best effect comes from white petunias, which love hot weather. They can be massed in garden beds, pots or hanging baskets and will give a long-lasting display. Tall white cosmos will flower from mid-summer through autumn if they are dead-headed regularly, and spider flower will eventually grow to almost 6 ft after being in flower for many weeks on end. White sweet alyssum can be used year round and in summer it looks light and cool in clumps between other plants. White floss flower can be used in the summer garden too, but it does not always perform as well as the blue varieties.

AMARANTHUS

Amaranthus

'MOLTEN FIRE' makes a splash of red that few flowers can match. The hotter the summer, the more brilliant the leaves will be.

THIS IS 'JOSEPH'S COAT,' aptly named for its many-hued blend of red, gold and purple, often with touches of green.

FEATURES

Common names for different varieties of amaranthus include Joseph's coat (*A. tricolor*), prince's feather (*A. hybridus* var. *erythrostachys*) and love-lies-bleeding (*A. caudatus*). Most amaranthus are grown for their colorful foliage but one species, love-lies-bleeding, has attractive long, red tassels of bloom. Leaves can be red, bronze, yellow and green, depending on the variety. Amaranthus is a tall plant growing to 4 ft. It is suitable for use in large gardens and as background planting for spectacular summer displays of annuals.

CONDITIONS

Climate Does not perform well in cool areas.
Aspect Prefers full sun all day and needs some protection from wind.
Soil Prefers well-drained soil. Prepare soil several weeks ahead of planting by digging in large amounts of well-decayed manure or compost. Apply all-purpose fertilizer to soil about one week before planting. For most benefit place fertilizer in a shallow trench 3–4 in deep where plants are to grow so that roots do not reach the fertilizer until the seedlings are fully established.

GROWING METHOD

Planting Grow from seed planted in middle to late spring or from purchased seedlings.
Watering Water well after planting. Once plants are established, water heavily once or twice a week, depending on soil and weather conditions. This develops a good root system, which is essential for a long-lasting display.
Fertilizing If soil has been well prepared, plants should not need feeding very often. Apply liquid fertilizer or bone meal once a month.
Problems Snails can be a problem when plants are young. Because the foliage is the main feature of this plant, watch for damage by chewing insects.

FLOWERING

Season In warm to hot weather plants should provide brilliant color in the garden from early summer to at least the middle of autumn.
Cutting Not really suitable for cutting as you need to cut down the whole plant to obtain the colorful foliage.

AFTER FLOWERING

General Once plants are finished, dig them out and chop them up for mulch or compost.

ANEMONE

Anemone coronaria

'ST BRIGID,' with semi-double flowers, is the best known strain of anemone. It is available in straight colors or mixtures.

JUST SOME OF THE COLORS available are shown here. The reds are brilliant but go surprisingly well with the soft blues and pinks.

FEATURES

The strong clear colors of anemones have great garden impact. The flowers can be singles ('de Caen' strain) or doubles ('St Brigid' strain) in blue, red, white, pink, cyclamen, and two-toned red and white or lavender and white. They are best grown as annuals but can sometimes flower a second year if tubers are left in the ground. Plants grow to 8–12 in.

CONDITIONS

Climate   Not suitable for tropical areas. Prefers a warm to cool climate.

Aspect   Needs at least half a day's sun and grows best in full sun with some wind protection.

Soil   Must have well-drained soil or tubers rot. Once plants have emerged, mulch around them with well-decayed manure or compost.

GROWING METHOD

Planting   Grow from seed sown in late summer, or more easily from tubers planted out from late summer to the middle of autumn. Plant tubers 1–1½ in deep and about 6 in apart.

Watering   Water thoroughly after planting but do not water again until shoots appear, unless the weather is very dry. Once shoots appear, water regularly but do not allow the soil to become at all soggy.

Fertilizing   Once flower stems/buds appear, give liquid fertilizer every two weeks.

Problems   No special problems.

FLOWERING

Season   Spring in most areas. In cool zones they may flower through to summer.

Cutting   Excellent cut flower. Cut stem with a sharp knife or shears to avoid damaging the plant. Flowers should last well if picked when buds first open.

AFTER FLOWERING

General   Continue to care for plants until the foliage yellows or dies down. Dig up the tubers, allow them to dry in the shade, and then clean and store them in an old stocking or net in a dry, airy place. They will keep well and can be planted out again next year.

ASTER

Callistephus chinensis

DOUBLE ASTERS such as this 'Giant Crego' have many admirers, although the single, daisy-type ones are also popular.

ASTERS make a great show even though their season isn't very long. Don't plant them in the same bed two years running.

FEATURES

A colorful plant for garden display and cutting, the aster grows to 16–24 in. Flowers are pink, blue, mauve, white, red and purple. Wilt-resistant varieties such as 'Giant Crego' produce strong, healthy plants. Asters are excellent flowers for cutting and are very popular with florists.

CONDITIONS

Climate Not suitable for very cold areas as they are very sensitive to frost.

Aspect Needs full sun and wind protection. Unsuitable for windy situations.

Soil Needs light, well-drained soil; not suitable for heavy soils. Add organic matter to soil several weeks ahead of planting.

Support Does not need support. Where wind is an occasional problem, plant 10–12 in apart so that plants support each other.

GROWING METHOD

Planting Sow seed early to middle spring. Fine seed should be covered very lightly. Seedlings are worth planting until the middle of summer.

Watering Water regularly. Aim to soak the soil rather than sprinkle.

Fertilizing Once plants are established, give side dressings of complete plant food monthly or soluble plant food every two weeks.

Problems May be attacked by a range of insect pests. Greening and distortion of flowers may be caused by big bud or virescence, death of the growing point by broad bean wilt. Both these diseases are carried by sap-sucking insects and there is no cure for them. Remove and destroy affected plants.

FLOWERING

Season Early summer to early autumn in most areas.

Cutting Excellent cut flower. It is very popular for use in mixed arrangements.

AFTER FLOWERING

General Dig plants out and add them to the mulch or compost if they are disease-free.

AURORA DAISY
Arctotis

HOT COLORS are a speciality of aurora daisies. Tawny red, as here, coral or gold are softened by the grayish foliage.

THESE SPREADING but low-growing plants are best used en masse as a groundcover. Here New Zealand flax provides contrast.

FEATURES

The aurora daisy is grown for its colorful daisy-type flowers, most commonly in pink, red or white, with black and yellow centers. Plants reach 12 in or more in height. This spreading plant is useful as a groundcover for large areas. It is often sold as a perennial but performs best if treated as an annual.

CONDITIONS

Climate   Tolerates a wide range of climates but does best where humidity is low. Not suitable for tropical areas.

Aspect   Needs full sun all day—flowers close in shade or on dull days. Sloping ground is ideal for these plants.

Soil   Prefers sandy soil with very good drainage. Dig in rotted compost or manure a few weeks before planting to help retain moisture during hot weather.

GROWING METHOD

Planting   Sow seed in late winter to early spring, or look for plants in the groundcover sections of your local nurseries.

Watering   Water regularly to establish plants, then give a heavy soaking about once a week.

Fertilizing   Performs well even in poor soil. If desired, apply pelleted poultry manure or bone meal when flower buds appear, but this is not essential for good flowers.

Problems   No special problems but heavy, poorly drained soils may cause root rot.

FLOWERING

Season   Spring to late summer.

Cutting   Not suitable as a cut flower—it has short stems and a tendency to close in poor light.

AFTER FLOWERING

General   The plant is best dug out after flowering but if desired you can try cutting it back hard to see whether it will carry through until the next flowering season.

BABY BLUE EYES

Nemophila menziesii

THE CHINA BLUE flowers have a distinctive white center. They bloom in such numbers they almost hide the leaves of this lovely plant.

THESE BABY BLUE EYES are set off by meadowfoam in a classic blue, white and gold color scheme.

FEATURES

Baby blue eyes has lovely china blue flowers with a white eye. A low-growing plant to 6–8 in, it makes a pretty border plant or a fine partner for spring bulb displays. To achieve the best display, plant the bulbs first and then sow the baby blue eyes seed around and between them.

CONDITIONS

Climate Unsuitable for very hot areas, it grows in warm areas but does best in cool regions.

Aspect Needs full sun to half shade.

Soil Needs well-drained soil; does not tolerate heavy clays. Adding organic matter to soil a few weeks ahead of planting improves the growing conditions.

GROWING METHOD

Planting Sow seed in late autumn or very early spring, where plants are to grow.

Watering Don't overwater if weather is cool and overcast. Regular deep watering about once a week should be sufficient unless weather is very dry and windy.

Fertilizing Apply a sprinkle of bone meal or pelleted poultry manure when buds appear. A soluble fertilizer applied every two weeks is also suitable for these plants.

Problems No particular problems but overwet, poorly drained soil causes plants to rot.

FLOWERING

Season Spring to summer. The floral display lasts longer in cooler areas.

Cutting Not suitable as a cut flower as the stems are very short.

AFTER FLOWERING

General Dig or pull out plants once they begin to look untidy. Sometimes they self-seed and so you may get a pleasant surprise the following year.

BABY'S BREATH

Gypsophila elegans

MOSTLY GROWN FOR CUTTING, baby's breath can also be used to make a lovely floating cloud of white flowers in the garden. The season is, however, short: if you want a display of any length at all, you will need to make successive sowings.

FEATURES

Attractive in the garden planted in drifts, baby's breath grows to 18–24 in high with fine stems bearing dainty pink, white or rose flowers. With its fine foliage and small flowers, it is widely used in floral work. The very tiny flowered variety is 'Bristol Fairy,' a cultivar of the perennial *G. paniculata*.

CONDITIONS

Climate   *G. paniculata* does best in cooler climates. *G. elegans* also prefers a cooler climate but it is possible to grow it in most areas except for tropical regions.

Aspect   Must have shelter from strong wind and prefers full sun.

Soil   Needs compost or manure for stronger plants and better flowering. In very acid soils needs the addition of lime before planting, about 3½ oz per square yard.

GROWING METHOD

Planting   In warm zones sow at any time of year, in cool zones from the middle of spring to late summer. Space plants 4–6 in apart to support each other.

Watering   Once plants are established, water them deeply once a week, and more often in very warm or windy weather.

Fertilizing   Not generally necessary if the soil has been well prepared.

Problems   No special problems.

FLOWERING

Season   Plants take 8–10 weeks to flower from seed and can be produced throughout the year in warm areas.

Cutting   Ideal cut flower. It can be used alone or to complement other flowers in a mixed arrangement.

AFTER FLOWERING

General   Pull out plants when flowers fade. When baby's breath is grown for florists, the flowers are not cut, but the plants are pulled out whole, roots and all.

BALSAM

Impatiens balsamina

THE BEST STRAINS of balsam have richly colored double flowers that are sometimes compared to small camellias.

BALSAM FLOWERS tend to hide in the leaves: the effect is of touches of bright color, particularly effective against other foliage plants.

FEATURES

Also known as busy lizzie, balsam is pretty for garden display, or it can be used in pots and troughs. It is less widely grown than the longer lasting *I. wallerana* but it has a wider range of flower forms. An erect annual, balsam grows to 24 in high, while dwarf forms grow to 10–12 in. Single and double flowers come in red, magenta, pink, white and yellow.

CONDITIONS

Climate Has no tolerance for cold conditions and should be grown only in warm to hot areas. May be started under glass in cool zones and planted out later.

Aspect Prefers full to half sun and protection from strong wind.

Soil Needs well-drained soil but no special preparation is necessary.

GROWING METHOD

Planting In warm areas sow in autumn or very early spring, in cool areas in spring when danger of frost has passed. Barely cover the very fine seed. Transplant into permanent position when seedlings are about 2 in high.

Watering Water regularly in dry weather but take care not to keep the soil wet or the stems will be sure to rot.

Fertilizing Apply bone meal or pelleted poultry manure once plants are growing strongly, but take care as too much fertilizer results in soft, sappy growth.

Problems No special problems. Overwatering causes rotting and plant collapse.

FLOWERING

Season Throughout warm weather (spring through summer months).

Cutting Not suitable as a cut flower, but potted plants in flower can be used as temporary indoor decoration if desired.

AFTER FLOWERING

General Discard plants when they begin to look unattractive. They may self-sow and reappear the following year but the range of form and color will probably not be the same.

BEGONIA

Begonia x semperflorens-cultorum

THERE ARE MANY STRAINS of wax begonias. This one, in red, pink and white, is called 'Fair Lady'.

BEGONIAS ARE first-rate container plants. Here a dwarf pale pink variety sets off a golden-leafed false cypress.

FEATURES

An excellent plant for beds or borders, pots, troughs and rockeries, begonias are soft-stemmed plants with somewhat waxy leaves. They form a mound-like shape 6–12 in high. Flowers are white, pink or red and can last for many months. Foliage is bronze or green. Begonias are perennials but for best effect are grown as annuals.

CONDITIONS

Climate   Prefers a warm climate and cannot be planted outdoors in cool zones unless there is a warm sheltered microclimate.

Aspect   Prefers morning sun, afternoon shade and protection from strong, drying wind. Dappled sunlight is also suitable but in too much shade plants grow leggy and thin.

Soil   Most garden soils are suitable but plants do not tolerate very heavy clays that stay wet for long periods.

GROWING METHOD

Planting   Seed is extremely fine and difficult to handle. Sow on the surface of the seed-starting mix and barely cover. Water from below so as not to disturb seed. Sow early spring to summer. Plant out 6–8 in apart when seedlings are large enough to handle.

Watering   Water regularly and deeply in dry weather but do not keep soil soggy.

Fertilizing   Once plants are growing strongly give complete plant food, granular or liquid, about once a month.

Problems   Overwatering causes plants to rot. Powdery mildew can sometimes be a problem. Avoid overhead watering as much as possible, don't overwater or water late in the day. Cyclamen mite can cause curling and distortion of new growth. This is extremely difficult to control, even using chemicals—it is probably best to destroy affected plants.

FLOWERING

Season   In optimum conditions flowers for many months from spring through autumn.

Cutting   Not suitable as a cut flower. Potted plants make good temporary indoor plants.

AFTER FLOWERING

General   Try cutting back plants after flowering is finished—you may get a second flush of growth and flower. Otherwise dig the plants out and discard them.

BELLS OF IRELAND

Molucella laevis

THE ACTUAL FLOWER *of the bells of Ireland is a tiny white affair, like a clapper in the green bell of the calyx.*

'BELLS OF IRELAND' *actually come from Syria. Here they are used in a very effective all-green scheme.*

FEATURES

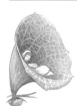

Also known as molucca balm, bells of Ireland is a lightly scented, tall-growing plant to 24–36 in. Its appearance gives no clue to the fact that it belongs to the mint family of plants. Bells of Ireland have shell-like green "flowers" that are actually the calyces. They can be grown for garden display, but they are mostly grown as a cut flower—they are very popular with flower arrangers for both the color and the form.

CONDITIONS

Climate	Tolerates a very wide range of climatic conditions.
Aspect	Needs an open, sunny site. Must have wind protection or tall stems will be damaged.
Soil	Tolerates wide range of soil types but must have good drainage. Adding manure or compost to the bed well ahead of sowing time improves results.
Support	Should not need support if plants are sheltered from wind.

GROWING METHOD

Planting	Sow directly into the ground where the plants are to grow in early spring. Space 12–16 in apart.

Watering	Water deeply in dry weather on a regular basis. Deep watering aids formation of good root mass to support this tall plant; shallow, frequent watering results in small, shallow roots so that plants tend to topple over.
Fertilizing	Apply little or no extra fertilizer if organic matter has already been added to the soil before planting.
Problems	No special problems.

FLOWERING

Season	Display is not long lasting but plants should flower in summer for a few weeks.
Cutting	Ideal cut flower. Cut when flowers are well formed. Florists remove leaves to display the green calyces better. Flowers dry to a light brown color but can still be used for decoration. Dried stems can also be used in floral arrangements.

AFTER FLOWERING

General	Remove plants once they are past their peak. Flowers maturing and drying on the plant frequently shed seed, which will germinate the following year.

BLACK-EYED SUSAN

Rudbeckia hirta

THE 'BLACK EYE' of the annual black-eyed Susan is the dark center of the daisy flower. The petals are in a range of warm colors to enliven the garden: as well as the tawny color seen here, they are available in bright shades of gold and orange.

FEATURES

Also known as coneflower and marmalade daisy, black-eyed Susan has large, daisy-type flowers with prominent dark centers in colors such as black, purple or green. The flowers are mostly in the yellow, orange and mahogany color range. Plants grow 30–36 in tall and are suitable for massed planting or use at the back of a floral border.

CONDITIONS

Climate Suitable for warm and cool zones. Cannot grow satisfactorily in the tropics.

Aspect Needs full sun all day and wind protection.

Soil Must have well-drained soil. Tolerates poor soil but performs better in soils containing some organic matter.

Support Support not needed if close planted in a sheltered spot. Pinch out tips when plants are 6–8 in high to encourage branching and sturdier plants.

GROWING METHOD

Planting Sow in spring; in cool zones delay until all danger of frost has passed. Sow in pots or directly into the ground. Direct sowings can be thinned to 12 in spacings and pot-grown seedlings transplanted when they are large enough to handle.

Watering Once plants are established, heavy weekly watering should be sufficient.

Fertilizing Not essential but a monthly application of complete plant food results in larger plants and flowers.

Problems No special problems.

FLOWERING

Season Summer and autumn. In cool zones where planting has been delayed, flowering is usually in autumn only.

Cutting Suitable for use as a cut flower.

AFTER FLOWERING

General Remove plants once they are past their best. They sometimes self-seed if flowers are left to age and die naturally on the plant.

BROWALLIA
Browallia speciosa

BROWALLIA FOLIAGE is quilted and rather glossy, making an effective frame for the delicate flowers with their white throats. The sprawling habit of these plants makes them an excellent choice for a hanging basket or tall container, or any spill-over situation.

FEATURES

Browallia is also known as amethyst flower or bush violet from its violet-blue flowers, which give a pleasing, cool effect in hot weather. Each flower has a contrasting white eye. Grows to about 12 in and is suitable for planting in garden beds, pots and hanging baskets. It should not be confused with the yellow/orange flowered shrub (*Streptosolen jamesonii*) also known as "browallia".

CONDITIONS

Climate   Not suitable for cool areas unless it is grown as an indoor plant.

Aspect   Needs at least half a day's sun and tolerates full sun. Requires warmth and shelter.

Soil   Not fussy about soil but does not tolerate poor drainage. Where drainage is poor or soil heavy, grow in pots or baskets.

GROWING METHOD

Planting   Sow in early spring in pots or trays. Don't cover the fine seed—it needs light to germinate. Water pots from below to avoid dislodging the seed. Transplant when large enough to handle.

Watering   Water regularly to establish. Once plants are established, water heavily less often. Once a week should be ample unless weather is very hot or windy.

Fertilizing   Apply occasional liquid feeds or granular fertilizer which may be beneficial if the soil is poor. Don't overfeed or your plants will be all leaves and few flowers.

Problems   No special problems.

FLOWERING

Season   Can flower for long periods in warm weather. Summer is the main flowering time but can flower at other times in favorable conditions.

Cutting   Not suitable as a cut flower.

AFTER FLOWERING

General   If plants still look good in autumn, try potting up one or two as indoor plants; otherwise discard them.

CALENDULA

Calendula officinalis

'SUNTIPS,' a new variety of calendula, shows some of the range of warm colors available. From a distance they blend to a golden effect.

BLUE AND GOLD is a time-honored color scheme: here calendulas provide the gold, lavender and Eranthemum pulchellum *the blue.*

FEATURES

Also known as pot marigold or English marigold, the calendula is a fast growing, bushy annual with many-petaled, daisy-type flowers in shades of yellow, orange and honey. The leaves, which have a slight scent, are light green in color. Usually grown in borders or in massed displays of annuals, they grow to 12–20 in.

CONDITIONS

Climate   Not suitable for the tropics but does well in most other climatic zones.

Aspect   Needs full sun for best results.

Soil   Tolerates wide range of soils and performs reasonably well even in poor soil. Adding organic matter to the soil ahead of planting time improves results. Calendula does not tolerate bad drainage.

GROWING METHOD

Planting   In most areas best results come from autumn sowings; in cool zones sow in spring and summer. Sow in pots or directly into the ground. Thin direct sowings later if seedlings are too crowded. Space plants 10–12 in apart.

Watering   Water regularly to develop large plants with good flowering potential and to maintain flowering during the season.

Fertilizing   Apply granular fertilizer alongside plants or occasional liquid fertilizer which will result in larger blooms. Don't apply fertilizer until plants are growing strongly and are quite well established.

Problems   Rust can be a serious problem—if it is severe, spray with a fungicide. Destroy self-sown seedlings as they are often a host for this disease. Powdery mildew can be a problem in some seasons. With both these fungal problems avoid overhead watering where possible and avoid watering late in the day. Aphids can sometimes cause problems—spray with an insecticidal soap or pyrethrum.

FLOWERING

Season   From late winter to spring. Longer flowering periods in cooler areas.

Cutting   Good cut flower, used widely in floral trade. Cutting flowers helps to lengthen flowering period. Cut when flowers are well formed but before petals open out too far.

AFTER FLOWERING

General   Remove plants and destroy or add to compost if they are quite healthy.

CALIFORNIAN POPPY

Eschscholzia californica

YELLOW CALIFORNIAN POPPIES are here combined in an unusual color scheme with the acid green of Euphorbia polychroma.

TWO CONTINENTS MEET in blue and gold with these golden Californian poppies and blue Swan River daisies.

FEATURES

The bright orange flowers and finely divided gray-green foliage of the Californian poppy look best when planted in large drifts, although it grows well even in crevices of rockeries. Other forms have flowers in yellow, cream, pink/beige and scarlet. They grow 12–20 in high and spread up to 20 in each way. They are named after the state of California, of which this plant is the floral emblem.

CONDITIONS

Climate   Not suitable for the tropics but does well in most other climatic zones.

Aspect   Must have full sun.

Soil   Needs well-drained soil to do well. Tolerates poor soil as long as drainage is good. No special preparation necessary.

GROWING METHOD

Planting   Sow where it is to grow as it is not easy to transplant. If sowings are too thick, seedlings can be thinned out later. Sow ¼ in or less deep. Take care not to dislodge seed when watering. Best sown during late winter or early spring.

Watering   Water regularly to establish but, once established, an occasional deep watering is all that is required. This is a drought-tolerant plant and is more likely to perform poorly if watered too frequently.

Fertilizing   Fertilizing is usually not necessary. Excess fertilizer results in excess leaf growth.

Problems   No particular pest or disease problems but overwatering causes plants to rot.

FLOWERING

Season   Long flowering period through the spring and summer months.

Cutting   May be used as a cut flower although flowers close at night. Cut long stems and place in water immediately.

AFTER FLOWERING

General   Plants may continue to look good but they are past their best and should be removed. They often self-seed and so seedlings can be expected the following season. Use chopped up plants as mulch or add to compost.

CALLIOPSIS
Coreopsis tinctoria

'BADENGOLD' is a perennial form of calliopsis but its color and form is also typical of annual calliopsis.

THE OPEN, AIRY HABIT of calliopsis offsets the brilliance of its color and makes it ideal for wild, informal styles of planting.

FEATURES

Cultivated calliopsis make good garden plants with single and double flowers in yellow, red and mahogany tones, growing to 20–36 in high. It is a very adaptable plant, growing almost anywhere. (In its native habitat it occurs in every extreme of climate.) The yellow-flowered calliopsis that grows wild (*C. lanceolata*) is a perennial.

CONDITIONS

Climate
Aspect   Does well in a wide range of climatic zones. Must have full sun and wind protection to give best results.

Soil   Tolerates poor soil but best results come where soil has been enriched with decayed manure or compost well ahead of planting time.

Support   Should not need support if planted in sheltered situations as plants tend to support each other.

GROWING METHOD

Planting   Sow seed in late spring or early summer in pots or where they are to grow. Space plants 8–12 in apart.

Watering   Water regularly to establish. Once established a weekly soaking should be ample unless weather is exceptionally hot and windy.

Fertilizing   Should not need supplementary fertilizer if soil has been well prepared.

Problems   No particular insect pest or disease problems. A very hardy plant in most circumstances. Overwatering in poorly drained soil could cause plant collapse.

FLOWERING

Season   Long flowering period through summer, especially if spent flowers are regularly removed from the plants.

Cutting   Can be used as a cut flower. Pick when the flowers have opened fully but the petals are still firm and fresh looking.

AFTER FLOWERING

General   Plants are best removed after flowering stops. There may be some self-sown seedlings the following year.

CANDYTUFT

Iberis umbellata

CANDYTUFT comes in a range of candy colors: light and bright pink and white as well as the pinky-mauve you see here.

WHITER THAN WHITE candytuft needs careful placing if it is not to look artificial. Set it off with greenery or rich deep colors.

FEATURES

A very decorative plant that grows to 12–16 in tall, candytuft is suitable for garden display and planting in troughs. Flowers range from white, pink and mauve to purple. A dwarf form, usually sold as 'Fairy Mixed', grows to only 8–10 in. Another species, *I. amara*, has pure white, fragrant flowers.

CONDITIONS

Climate   Tolerates a wide range of climatic conditions.
Aspect   Needs a warm, sunny spot.
Soil   Prepare soil by adding well-decayed manure or compost a few weeks ahead of planting. Mix lime or dolomite, about 3½ oz per square yard, into the soil about one week before planting. Well-drained soil is essential as these plants do not tolerate heavy and/or poorly drained conditions.

GROWING METHOD

Planting   Best planted where they are to grow as they are not easy to transplant. If sowing in pots, use small pots to minimize disturbance when transplanting. Space 6–8 in apart to give best display. Sow in autumn in most areas but in cold zones sow in spring.

Watering   Water regularly to establish, but once established a heavy watering about once a week is all that is needed. Plants do not tolerate waterlogged soil.
Fertilizing   Apply granular or liquid complete plant food monthly to produce strong plants and abundant flowers.
Problems   No particular problems if growing conditions are suitable.

FLOWERING

Season   Flowers in spring and summer; *I. amara* usually flowers in middle to late spring.
Cutting   Good cut flower. Flowers that are well formed but not overmature should last well if picked early in the day and immediately plunged into water to soak before arranging.

AFTER FLOWERING

General   Remove plants after flowering. Some self-sown seedlings may appear the following season.

HINT

Alternatives   There are a number of annual and perennial candytufts other than those described here. One of the best garden plants is the perennial *I. sempervirens*, which has stunning chalk white flowers. It rarely grows more than 10 in high and makes a fine border plant.

CANTERBURY BELLS

Campanula medium

WHITE CANTERBURY BELLS are here mixed with blue floss flower and the contrast in form and color is just about perfect.

THERE ARE ALSO PERENNIAL forms of Canterbury bells, such as these bats-in-the-belfry, Campanula trachelium.

FEATURES

Also known as bellflowers, Canterbury bells are a classic component of the cottage-style garden. They are best in massed plantings in borders or among shrubs. Characteristic are the large, bell-shaped flowers in blue, pink, mauve or white, which grow on stems 28–32 in high. Grown as biennials in cool climates, Canterbury bells are best grown as annuals in temperate areas.

CONDITIONS

Climate   Prefers cool or warm zones. Not suitable for the tropics or hot, dry regions.

Aspect   Grows in full sun or part shade but does need wind protection.

Soil   Needs plenty of well-rotted manure or compost dug into the soil ahead of planting. Requires good drainage but the soil should retain some moisture between waterings. It should not dry out.

Support   Support not needed in early stages of plant development but light staking may be necessary when plants are in bloom.

GROWING METHOD

Planting   Sow the very fine seed in late summer or early autumn in pots or trays. Barely cover seed and water from below to avoid disturbing it. Plant out at about 12 in intervals when seedlings are large enough to handle.

Watering   Keep soil just moist in dry weather by watering heavily once or twice a week, depending on weather conditions. Soil rich in organic matter helps retain moisture.

Fertilizing   Once plants are established, give them a monthly application of complete plant food, in granular or liquid form.

Problems   No particular pest or disease problems.

FLOWERING

Season   Middle to late spring is the normal flowering period but in cool areas they may flower into the summer months.

Cutting   May be used as a cut flower but you may get more pleasure from its garden display.

AFTER FLOWERING

General   Remove plants after the flowering season and add them to mulch or compost.

CINERARIA
Senecio x *hybridus*

CINERARIA LEAVES are not particularly beautiful but they set off the great domes of richly colored daisies to perfection.

CINERARIA FLOWERS are generally dark and they ought to look somber in the shade, but they don't. They look velvety and sumptuous.

FEATURES

These showy plants with clustered heads of daisy-like flowers grow to 20 in high, while dwarf forms reach 6–8 in. A large color range includes crimson, purple, royal blue, pink, lavender, white and bicolors. It makes a spectacular garden display and is suitable for pots and troughs. Potted plants are often sold for temporary indoor decoration.

CONDITIONS

Climate Suitable for growing outdoors in warm or tropical areas only. Often grown for green house display in cool areas.

Aspect Prefers shade and shelter from strong wind; does not tolerate frost.

Soil Well-drained soil with organic matter added beforehand should produce good results.

GROWING METHOD

Planting Sow seeds in late summer to autumn. In cool zones raise plants in green houses or under cover. In all areas seeds are best sown in pots or trays and barely covered with seed-starting mix. When large enough to handle, plant them out at 12 in intervals for tall varieties and 8 in spacings for dwarf forms. If growing cinerarias in containers, pot them up initially into very small pots and gradually increase pot size as they develop.

Watering Once plants are established, a heavy watering once a week should be sufficient unless the weather is extremely dry and windy.

Fertilizing Apply all-purpose plant food monthly during the growing season. Once buds appear, apply liquid fertilizer every 10–14 days. Make sure soil is moist before applying fertilizer.

Problems Leaf miner can be a problem but it does not spoil flowering. This pest cannot be controlled without the use of a systemic insecticide and unless your garden is on display, you can probably ignore it. Aphids sometimes attack the new growth—wash them off with the hose or spray with an insecticidal soap. Powdery mildew can be a problem in some seasons.

FLOWERING

Season Late winter and early spring.

Cutting Flowers may be used as cut flowers but this is not usual. Potted cinerarias in flower make a good cut flower substitute, both indoors and in outdoor living areas.

AFTER FLOWERING

General Remove plants once the flowers have faded.

COCKSCOMB

Celosia cristata

THE FEATHERY FLOWER HEADS of cockscombs are made up of many flowers, each too small to be significant on its own.

THE BRILLIANT COLORS of cockscomb always look best with plenty of accompanying greenery to mask their rather dowdy foliage.

FEATURES

Also known as Prince of Wales feathers or feathery amaranth, cockscomb has plume-like flowers ranging from deep crimson and scarlet to orange and golden yellow. The tall forms grow to 30 in, the dwarf forms to 10–12 in. Cockscomb is often used in large-scale plantings in parks and public gardens but is just as effective in home gardens.

CONDITIONS

Climate Not suitable for very cold areas; does best in warm and even tropical zones.
Aspect Must have full sun all day for best results.
Soil Needs well-drained soil that has been enriched with well-decayed manure or compost. Good soil preparation is essential to maintain the plants over their long flowering period.

GROWING METHOD

Planting In warm areas sow seed during spring. Sow seed in pots or trays, lightly covered with seed-starting mix. Transplant when large enough to handle, spacing tall forms 12–15 in apart and dwarf forms 6–8 in apart.

Watering Once plants are established, reduce watering to a heavy soaking once a week although you may need to water more often in very hot, windy weather. Mulching will help to retain moisture during very hot weather.
Fertilizing Supplementary fertilizing is probably not necessary if soil has been well prepared.
Problems No particular problems.

FLOWERING

Season Long flowering period through summer and autumn months.
Cutting May be used as a cut flower for unusual indoor decoration. Cut plumes and hang them upside down in a dry, airy place for later use in dried flower arrangements.

AFTER FLOWERING

General Remove plants and either discard them or chop them up and add the pieces to your compost or use as mulch.

COLEUS

Solenostemon scutellarioides, syn. *Coleus* x *hybridus*

SEEMINGLY INFINITE *variations of color and form are the main characteristic of coleus. Propagate your favorites by taking cuttings.*

SMALL BLUE FLOWERS *add little to the coleus display—it's usual to trim off the flower spikes but it's not compulsory.*

FEATURES

The most striking aspect of the coleus, also called flame nettle or painted leaves, is its soft-textured, multi-colored leaves in a large range of colors. It can be grown as a short-lived perennial in warm climates but to achieve the best display it should be grown as an annual. It is useful as a background plant in floral borders, but is also effective as a filler between shrubs or as a pot plant.

CONDITIONS

Climate   Grows outdoor in warm climates only as it has no tolerance for cold conditions.

Aspect   Prefers a warm, sheltered, partly shaded position but tolerates full sun as long as there is ample moisture.

Soil   Needs well-drained soil that has a high organic content.

Support   Plants grown in a sheltered spot should not need staking.

GROWING METHOD

Planting   Easily grown from soft-tip cuttings but plants can also be raised from seed. Sow the seed in late winter or early spring on seed-starting mix and do not cover it. Keep the mix just moist until the seedlings appear. Thin out the seedlings and plant them out when they are large enough to handle into garden beds or small pots. For garden display space out 10–12 in apart.

Watering   Needs regular, copious supplies of water to maintain growth or leaves will be small and growth stunted.

Fertilizing   Give regular liquid feeding throughout the growing season to maintain vigorous leaf growth, especially as this is the main attraction of these plants.

Problems   No particular problems. Watch for slugs and snails on small plants.

FLOWERING

Season   Flowers are usually blue or purple but are insignificant. They should be removed as soon as they appear in summer. Once plants have flowered, leaf growth stops.

Cutting   Foliage can be used in floral displays but is not very satisfactory.

AFTER FLOWERING

General   In warm areas you may leave plants in the ground for another year or two but you will not get the same display of lush foliage without a good deal of care. Plants would need to be cut back hard, then given copious watering and fertilizing in the following spring and summer to try to produce vigorous growth. Plants are probably best discarded but you can perpetuate your favorite plants by taking cuttings.

COLUMBINE
Aquilegia x *hybrida*

THE LONG-SPURRED columbine hybrids are admired for their airy grace. They come in every color of the rainbow.

THE OLD-FASHIONED granny's bonnet, Aquilegia vulgaris, *has short, curled spurs. It is denser and bushier than the long-spurred types.*

FEATURES

Columbines are also known as granny's bonnets. Their charming flowers and attractive foliage are delightful. Perennial in cold climates but best treated as annuals in temperate areas, they grow 16–28 in tall. Modern hybrids have long-spurred flowers in a wide color range, which includes white, pink, crimson, yellow, blue and various pastel combinations. Older forms and species are short spurred and more truly resemble an old-fashioned bonnet. The cultivar 'Nora Barlow,' which has red, pink and green shades in the flower, is an especially interesting form.

CONDITIONS

Climate Not suitable for tropics or arid regions.
Aspect Needs full sun in cool areas, part shade in warm areas, with some wind protection.
Soil Prefers well-drained soil enriched with manure or compost before planting.

GROWING METHOD

Planting Sow seed in autumn in pots or directly into the garden; in cold areas plant in late spring. Space seeds 12 in apart.
Watering Needs regular deep watering to encourage good root growth. In dry, windy weather ensure plants don't dry out.
Fertilizing Supplementary fertilizer is generally not needed if soil has been well prepared.
Problems No special problems.

FLOWERING

Season The middle of spring to early summer in warm areas; flowers may continue most of summer in cool zones.
Cutting Useful as a cut flower, with the gray-green maidenhair-like foliage being a great asset.

AFTER FLOWERING

General After foliage starts to die off, cut off at ground level. You may get a second year from plants. If flowers have dried on plants there may be seedlings the following year.

CONEFLOWER

Echinacea purpurea

THE CONE-SHAPED CENTER of the flower head gives this plant its common name. It can grow quite tall as the flowers age.

THE PINK FLOWERS are quite a soft color of magenta, but if you are really timid there is also a white variety.

FEATURES

Coneflowers are distinguished by their tall, sunflower-like flowers in a distinctive rich dusty pink color with black, cone-shaped centers. The plants have upright stems, with pointed leaves. They grow to 3 ft high and are suitable for massed planting, or they can be put at the back of borders or beds.

CONDITIONS

Climate Drought resistant. Tolerates most climatic conditions although unsuitable for growing in tropical regions.

Aspect Needs full sun all day and wind protection.

Soil Must have very well-drained soil. No special soil preparation is necessary.

Support Light staking is necessary when grown in windy situations, but the plants are self-supporting when they are mass planted in sheltered sites.

GROWING METHOD

Planting Sow seed in spring where plants are to grow or in pots. Transplant when 2 in high; space about 12 in apart.

Watering Water regularly to establish. Once plants are established, give an occasional deep soaking. Very tolerant of dry conditions.

Fertilizing Liquid or granular fertilizer once a month should be sufficient.

Problems No special problems.

FLOWERING

Season Summer into early autumn. Good garden display over many weeks.

Cutting Very good cut flower. Cut when flowers are fully formed but before the petals separate out too far.

AFTER FLOWERING

General Remove plants once flowering is finished. Flowers may self-seed if they are left to age and die on the plants, with new seedlings appearing the following year.

CORN COCKLE

Agrostemma githago

SOFT PINK 'Milas' is the oldest and best known of the corn cockle varieties. Deep pink and white are available, too.

CORN COCKLES look best in masses, spaced closely for their mutual support. Individual plants are rather flimsy.

FEATURES

Ideal for use in meadow gardens, corn cockles grow to 3 ft high on multi-stemmed growth. The large pink and white flowers open in wide trumpet shapes. They are suitable for use in massed planting or at the back of borders. Do take care, however, as the tiny dark corn cockle seeds are poisonous.

CONDITIONS

Climate   Grows in warm to cool areas. Unsuitable for tropical regions.
Aspect   Needs full sun and wind protection.
Soil   Tolerates most soil conditions but not heavy clay that stays wet for long periods after rain. No special soil preparation needed.
Support   Light staking is necessary if plants are grown in windy situations.

GROWING METHOD

Planting   Sow in autumn or very early spring where plants are to grow. Space the seed about 10–12 in apart.

Watering   Once established, heavy watering every week to ten days should be sufficient.
Fertilizing   Not generally necessary but if desired you can give complete plant food when flower buds begin to form.
Problems   No special problems.

FLOWERING

Season   Late spring to early summer.
Cutting   Cut when the flowers first open to obtain the best results.

AFTER FLOWERING

General   Remove plants once flowering is finished. They may have self-seeded to produce seedlings for the following year. If growing corn cockle in rural areas, take care to remove the plants before they produce seed as they can create a severe weed problem there if they are not controlled.

CORNFLOWER
Centaurea cyanus

CORNFLOWERS have a rather short season of bloom. Plant them among other flowers that will carry on the display.

BLUE AND WHITE is always a delightful combination. Here the blue cornflowers are planted with white roses.

FEATURES

The vibrant blue cornflowers with their branching stems make a great impact in massed plantings or garden displays. Intense "cornflower" blue is the most common color but mixtures that include white, pink and a paler blue are also available. Tall forms grow to 36 in, dwarf forms to 12 in.

CONDITIONS

Climate   Can be grown in warm to cool zones. Unsuitable for tropical regions.

Aspect   Prefers full sun but manages with half a day's sun. Protect tall varieties from wind.

Soil   Prepare soil by incorporating well-decayed organic matter three or four weeks before planting time.

GROWING METHOD

Planting   Sow in pots or directly where plants are to grow in autumn to early winter; in cool areas sow in late winter. Space the seeds 6–8 in apart. Thin direct sowings later if necessary.

Watering   A deep, weekly soaking should be enough once plants are established.

Fertilizing   Fertilize with complete plant food at the end of winter to encourage good flowering.

Problems   No special problems but plants are sometimes attacked by aphids in dry weather. Hose down foliage to reduce the numbers.

FLOWERING

Season   Late spring in most areas but into summer in cool zones.

Cutting   Excellent cut flower. Popular in arrangements or alone. Pick early in the day and scald stems before arranging in cool water.

AFTER FLOWERING

General   Remove plants once flowering stops. Cornflowers occasionally self-sow to produce plants the following year.

COSMOS
Cosmos bipinnatus

FINELY CUT FOLIAGE is a beautiful foil for the symmetrical flowers of 'Sensation Mixed,' a tall-growing cosmos variety.

WHITE COSMOS, set off by their own leaves and other greenery, create a refreshingly cool picture on a hot summer day.

FEATURES

Best planted in drifts or as background plants in mixed borders, these tall plants reach 5 ft high, with finely cut, feathery foliage and large daisy-type flowers. Red, cyclamen, pink and white are the most common colors but yellow, orange and scarlet varieties are available, too.

CONDITIONS

Climate	Can be grown in warm to cool zones. Unsuitable for tropical areas.
Aspect	Needs full sun to flourish, with some protection from wind.
Soil	Needs well-drained soil that is not enriched. Once seedlings are well established, mulch with rotted compost or manure.
Support	Support is not necessary if planted in a sheltered position.

GROWING METHOD

Planting	Sow in spring directly into the ground where plants are to grow. Cover with ¼ in of soil. Seed germinates in a few days. Frost tender, so don't sow before late spring in cool zones. Space plants 12–15 in apart.

Watering	Heavy weekly watering should be enough if the soil is mulched, unless the weather is very hot and dry. In sandy soils you may need to water twice weekly.
Fertilizing	Generally not necessary.
Problems	No special problems.

FLOWERING

Season	The middle of summer to autumn if spent flowers are removed regularly. In cool zones in late summer only.
Cutting	Ideal cut flower. Even a few of these bright flowers are very decorative.

AFTER FLOWERING

General	Remove plants in late autumn or when they begin to look untidy. Cosmos often self-seeds, and so leave some flowers on the plants to age and dry. The following year's flowers may not be as varied in color.

DAHLIA
Dahlia

BEDDING DAHLIAS are available in mixed or straight colors. This white variety has native violets as groundcover.

TALL-GROWING CACTUS DAHLIAS are so called from their quilled petals, which look a little like cactus flowers.

FEATURES

Dahlias form a bright multi-colored display in the garden or in large tubs and troughs. They are best known for the extensive range of herbaceous types grown from a swollen rootstock or tuber. Annual bedding dahlias grow to 15–30 in. Colors tend to be bright red, yellow, orange and pink.

CONDITIONS

Climate Can be grown in cool and warm regions. Unsuitable for tropical areas.

Aspect Needs full sun all day for best results.

Soil Needs well-drained soil. Dahlias are very heavy feeders and so dig in large amounts of decayed manure or compost at least two or three weeks before planting.

GROWING METHOD

Planting Sow seed in spring in trays or directly into the ground, covered by about 1/8 in of soil. Water thoroughly after sowing but avoid dislodging seed.

Watering Once seedlings are growing strongly, water heavily once or twice a week, depending on the soil and weather conditions. Continue watering regularly throughout the whole growing season.

Fertilizing Apply complete plant food once seedlings are 4–6 in high and continue to fertilize monthly. If you are using liquid fertilizer, apply it every two weeks.

Problems Dahlia leaves and flowers are very attractive to snails. Flowers may be chewed by grasshoppers and weevils. Powdery mildew and gray mold may be problems in humid weather. New growth may be distorted by mites and some virus diseases. Pull out any plants that appear to have abnormal growth.

FLOWERING

Season Summer and autumn—a long display, especially if plants are dead-headed often.

Cutting Excellent cut flower. If cut when flowers first open fully they should last seven to ten days with water changes.

AFTER FLOWERING

General Remove plants. If there is an especially outstanding plant, leave it to die down naturally. It may have formed a tuber that can be replanted the following year: take care to dig carefully.

DELPHINIUM

Delphinium x *cultorum*

'PACIFIC GIANTS' is the most popular strain of delphinium. It comes in a range of colors as well as the blue seen here.

A MIXED BORDER of delphiniums. The plant with the dark leaves is a ligularia, a herbaceous perennial.

FEATURES

An essential feature of a cottage garden, these tall, stately plants bear spires of blue, pink, lavender or white flowers up to 3 ft high. Perennial in cool climates, they are best grown as an annual in warmer areas. Use them as background plants in mixed borders or massed where height is needed.

CONDITIONS

Climate Best in cool zones but can also be grown in warm areas.

Aspect Prefers full sun but tolerates half a day's sun. Needs shelter from strong wind.

Soil Needs well-drained soil enriched with organic matter. Once plants are established, mulch generously with well-rotted manure or compost for a cool root run.

Support Light staking is necessary if plants are grown in a windy situation.

GROWING METHOD

Planting In warm zones sow in autumn; in cool zones sow in autumn under cover or in spring. Sow in pots or trays and plant out at 12–15 in intervals when large enough to handle.

Watering Needs regular deep watering to produce strong growth but the soil should never become waterlogged.

Fertilizing Once plants are 6–8 in high, fertilize monthly with granular or liquid complete plant food until buds form.

Problems No particular problems.

FLOWERING

Season In warm zones spring and early summer; in cool zones middle to late summer.

Cutting Excellent cut flower. Cut when the lowest flowers on the spike are fully open and the top buds are starting to show color.

AFTER FLOWERING

General In warm zones remove plants after they flower. In cool zones they may be left to die down naturally as you may get a second season's flowering from them. If retaining plants, cut off the foliage as it browns.

DIANTHUS
Dianthus chinensis

SINGLE-FLOWERED dianthus are less striking individually than the doubles, but they make a brighter mass display. This is 'Coral Rose,' a lovely bright, compact plant that makes a fine border for a garden bed or path.

FEATURES

Unlike other members of the carnation family, this short, tufty plant is only slightly scented. It has gray-green leaves and single and double flowers in mixed colors, including red, and red and white bicolors. Growing 8–12 in high, it is suitable for massed planting, edging garden beds, or for use in troughs or pots.

CONDITIONS

Climate   Performs best in cool zones but is also suitable for warm areas.
Aspect   Needs full sun.
Soil   Needs well-drained soil. Apply a light dressing of lime up to 3½ oz per square yard before planting.

GROWING METHOD

Planting   Best results from autumn sowing. Cover seed with no more than ¼ in of soil. When seedlings are 1–2 in high, space them out at 6 in intervals where they are to grow.

Watering   Don't overwater. Unless the weather is very dry, warm or windy a good weekly watering should be sufficient.
Fertilizing   Don't overfeed these plants. Complete plant food applied once or twice during the growing season is enough.
Problems   No special problems but overwatering will cause fairly rapid yellowing and rotting of these plants.

FLOWERING

Season   Late winter to the middle of spring. May flower from spring to the middle of summer in cool zones.
Cutting   Not as long lasting as carnations but can be useful in small arrangements.

AFTER FLOWERING

General   Cut back as there may be a second flowering but dianthus are rarely very good the second time around. It is probably best to remove them and replant next season.

DUSTY MILLER

Senecio cineraria

THE SILVER-DUSTED EFFECT of these intricately shaped leaves comes from the velvet-like hairs that cover them.

A FINE CLUMP of dusty miller in flower. Most gardeners prefer to cut off the flowers to encourage leaf growth.

FEATURES

Grown primarily for its attractive silver-gray foliage, rather than its yellow flowers, dusty miller is useful as an accent plant or edging for borders. It is often used in formal bedding schemes but looks equally effective in informal or cottage-style schemes. The plant grows to 12–18 in high.

CONDITIONS

Climate	Grows well in cool to warm areas.
Aspect	Must have full sun.
Soil	Must have well-drained soil. Does not need rich soil.

GROWING METHOD

Planting	Sow seed in late winter to early spring, in pots or directly in the ground. Cover with about ¼ in of soil. Can also be rooted from cuttings of the firm central growth.
Watering	Water regularly to establish but then restrict watering to a good soaking once every week or ten days.

Fertilizing	Not generally necessary but some bone meal or pelleted poultry manure can be applied when plants are 4–6 in high.
Problems	No special problems but poorly drained soils or overwatering causes root rots and eventual death of plants.

FLOWERING

Season	Yellow daisy-type flowers appear in late spring and early summer. The flowers are usually removed to allow leaf growth to continue.
Cutting	Foliage can be used most successfully in arrangements. Cut and soak the base of the stem before arranging.

AFTER FLOWERING

General	After flowers are removed, plants may continue to grow. They can be left in the garden while they are looking good, or they can be removed and fresh plants started next season.

ENGLISH DAISY

Bellis perennis

GARDENERS HAVE DEVELOPED *many forms and colors from the original tiny white English daisy. This is one.*

CRIMSON DAISIES *with gold centers here make an effective contrast with the blue violas at the edge of the bed.*

FEATURES

Perfect as a border plant with taller annuals or shrubs, English daisy is also suitable for rockeries, tubs and troughs. It is grown as a perennial in some cool climates but is best treated as an annual in more temperate areas. The low-growing, spreading plant grows 4–6 in high with white, pink, red or bicolor daisy flowers.

CONDITIONS

Climate   Not suitable for the tropics or for the hottest climates.

Aspect   Prefers full sun but tolerates some shade.

Soil   Most garden soils are suitable. Adding well-rotted manure or compost several weeks ahead of planting should increase plant vigor and flower size. Mulching to conserve moisture is beneficial if spring months are dry.

GROWING METHOD

Planting   Sow seed from autumn to early spring. Barely cover the small seed. Once plants are large enough to handle, space them 4–6 in apart in their permanent positions.

Watering   Give thorough watering regularly once plants are established. Heavy watering less often is better than frequent light sprinkles.

Fertilizing   With good soil preparation plants should need little fertilizer. Liquid fertilizer could be used every three or four weeks if you wish.

Problems   Rust can be a problem in some seasons. This plant is considered to be almost a weed in some areas.

FLOWERING

Season   Flowers from spring into early summer, longer in cool areas. Regular removal of spent flowers helps prolong the flowering period.

Cutting   Flowers make a lovely arrangement either alone or mixed with other small flowers.

AFTER FLOWERING

General   In warm areas pull plants out and discard them. In cool areas plants can be left to flower again the following year.

EVENING PRIMROSE

Oenothera rosea

MANY SPECIES of evening primrose stay open all day. This pink variety is one, and there is also an attractive white form.

ROMANTIC COLOR SCHEMES are easy with the soft color of evening primrose. Here it sets off marguerite daisies.

FEATURES

Evening primrose, also known as suncups, has prettily marked pink flowers and grows 12–16 in tall. It makes a lovely massed planting and is especially suitable for cottage-style gardens. It is slightly invasive as it grows from running roots as well as seeding but this species is well worth growing for its abundant flowers. It may be worth avoiding another species, *O. biennis*, which has become naturalized in many parts of the world and is a troublesome weed in some places.

CONDITIONS

Climate Can be grown well in warm to cool areas.
Aspect Full sun is best but half a day's direct sun is usually enough.
Soil Any reasonably well-drained soil suits. No special soil preparation is necessary.

GROWING METHOD

Planting Sow in late summer or autumn. Space plants 6–8 in apart for best display. Sow directly into the ground or into pots.

Watering Needs regular deep watering to promote good growth and to prolong flower display. Does not perform well if short of water.
Fertilizing Scatter pelleted poultry manure or complete plant food around plants once or twice during the growing season to ensure good results.
Problems No special problems.

FLOWERING

Season Flowers from spring into early summer in good conditions.
Cutting Does not perform very well as a cut flower.

AFTER FLOWERING

General If space allows, keep some plants for the following year. However, they will have started to spread; you will have to remove plants that invade areas where they are not wanted.

EVERLASTING DAISY

Helipterum roseum

MAINLY GROWN for cutting, everlasting daisies also make as bright a show in the garden as anyone could wish.

EVERLASTING DAISIES can be rather flimsy plants and they are best grown in drifts and clumps for mutual support.

FEATURES

The papery flowers of everlasting daisies come mainly in pinks and white. Reaching about 14–18 in tall, they are grown for garden display and are often used in dried arrangements. In areas of low rainfall where water is scarce, these daisies are the perfect choice to provide a long lasting floral display.

CONDITIONS

Climate   May not perform well in very humid areas. Best suited to warm or cool areas where humidity is low.

Aspect   Must have full sun.

Soil   Must have perfectly drained soil. Does not require rich soil and so no special preparation is necessary.

GROWING METHOD

Planting   Sow seed in autumn or spring but best results are from autumn sowing. Sow direct into the garden and cover lightly. Space seeds about 6–8 in apart.

Watering   Water regularly to establish seedlings but once plants are growing strongly water heavily only when soil has begun to dry out.

Fertilizing   Half-strength liquid fertilizer may be used every two weeks once plants are established but it is not essential.

Problems   No particular problems. Overwatering and poor drainage quickly kills plants.

FLOWERING

Season   Should flower about eight weeks after sowing. Display is long lasting.

Cutting   Ideal cut flower. Best cut and dried by hanging bunches upside down in a dry, airy place. Pick when flower petals are still rounded in towards the center.

AFTER FLOWERING

General   Remove and discard plants. In dry areas they may self-seed if some flowers are left to age and die on the plants.

EXHIBITION BORDER

Alternanthera ficoidea var. *amoena,* syn. *A. bettzichiana*

BRIGHTLY COLORED LEAVES are the point of this plant: the tiny whitish flowers pass unnoticed.

EXHIBITION BORDER is here used in the Victorian manner, as an edging to white petunias and more colored leaves, this time coleus.

FEATURES

Also known as copper leaf or Joseph's coat, exhibition border is a small edging plant that is grown for its foliage—green leaves splashed with red or cream. The flowers are insignificant. It is used extensively in parks and larger gardens in formal bedding schemes. It grows to 8 in high.

CONDITIONS

Climate   Needs tropical or warm conditions for the best growing results.
Aspect   Prefers full sun but tolerates half a day's sun.
Soil   Needs well-drained soil enriched with manure or compost before planting.

GROWING METHOD

Planting   Sow seed in autumn or spring in pots or trays. Plant out at 6–8 in intervals when plants are 1–2 in high.
Watering   Once established, this plant does best with a heavy weekly soaking rather than frequent light watering.

Fertilizing   Bone meal or pelleted poultry manure may be given once or twice during the growing season but is not essential.
Problems   No special problems.

FLOWERING

Season   In summer, but flowers are insignificant—the plant is grown for its foliage effect.
Cutting   Unsuitable for cutting.

AFTER FLOWERING

General   Trim lightly to remove flowers so that plants continue to grow. Remove plants once they begin to look thin and rangy.

HINT

Trimming   To make a more compact, formal border, trim lightly at any time during growth.

FLOSS FLOWER

Ageratum houstonianum

THESE FLUFFY FLOWERS are in fact daisies, without the ray petals. Colors range from blue to rich pink.

PINK AND BLUE floss flowers make a lovely grouping. The tall varieties are excellent cut flowers, lasting several days in the vase.

FEATURES

Fluffy flowers in blue, pink-mauve or white are characteristic of the floss flower. If the planting is timed to produce summer flowering, the cool colors will be particularly welcome. Tall forms grow to 20 in, dwarf forms to 6–8 in. The dwarf forms make good edging plants.

CONDITIONS

Climate Not suitable for very cold areas; does well in warm or tropical areas.

Aspect Prefers full sun but tolerates some shade.

Soil Prefers well-drained soil enriched with manure or compost well ahead of planting.

GROWING METHOD

Planting In warm zones sow in autumn or late winter, in cool zones in middle to late spring. Sow in pots or trays, lightly cover seed and transplant when 1–2 in high. Space tall varieties 10–12 in apart, and dwarf types 4–6 in apart.

Watering Keep soil just moist but not soggy throughout the growing season. Mulching will help to retain moisture.

Fertilizing Apply liquid or granular fertilizer monthly to maintain good growth.

Problems Aphids and whiteflies are sometimes a problem. Hose off or spray with pyrethrum or an insecticidal soap.

FLOWERING

Season Autumn sowings produce flowers in late winter and spring. Late winter sowings flower through late spring and summer. Cool zone plantings will flower in late summer and autumn.

Cutting Can be used as a cut flower if stems are scalded after picking and soaked in cool water before they are arranged.

AFTER FLOWERING

General Prune if desired as you may get a second flowering. Remove plants after flowering. They sometimes self-seed.

FORGET-ME-NOT

Myosotis sylvatica

EACH TINY FORGET-ME-NOT flower has a jeweled heart of silver and gold. They bloom in distinctive spiralled clusters.

A STUDY IN PALE BLUE—sky blue forget-me-nots and a single plant of pale blue Primula obconica.

FEATURES

When grown under trees, forget-me-not creates a natural woodland atmosphere. It reaches 10–14 in with small, sky blue flowers and rounded, bright green leaves. White and pink forms are also available. Often naturalized in gardens, the plants can be used in massed plantings or as fillers between shrubs as well as groundcover under trees.

CONDITIONS

Climate   Grows well in cool to warm regions. Not suitable for tropical areas.

Aspect   Grows in sun or shade. Suits dappled sunlight under deciduous trees and other sheltered sites.

Soil   Tolerates most soil conditions; responds well to soil with high organic content.

GROWING METHOD

Planting   Easily raised from seed sown direct into the ground or into pots in late summer and autumn. Space 6–8 in apart.

Watering   Give regular watering for best results. A good weekly soaking should be enough except in very windy, dry weather.

Fertilizing   Not necessary, but a sprinkle of bone meal or pelleted poultry manure improves vigor. Don't overfertilize or leaf growth will be too vigorous.

Problems   No special pest or disease problems. Occasionally shows a little powdery mildew on leaves but this is not worth treating.

FLOWERING

Season   Late winter and spring.

Cutting   Good for cutting. Lovely as a filler in larger arrangements and in small bouquets.

AFTER FLOWERING

General   Pull out plants when they begin to look untidy. They will have self-sown and the hooked seeds cling to everything. You may find forget-me-nots coming up in all kinds of places in the garden.

FOXGLOVE
Digitalis purpurea

OLD-FASHIONED purple foxgloves here grow in a cottage garden mix with red poppies and white rose mallow.

WHITE FOXGLOVES should not be grown with the purple ones, as they will cross with them and eventually all seedlings will be purple.

FEATURES

An essential part of the cottage garden, this biennial is often included with annuals. It grows to 3 ft or so, with spires of bell-shaped flowers in pink, white, magenta, cream or purple, with a spotted lip on each flower. Foxglove is best planted in groups as background plants, in borders or under tall trees that provide shelter. All parts of the plant are poisonous.

CONDITIONS

Climate   Grows well in cool and warm regions. Not suitable for tropical areas.

Aspect   Grows in half a day's sun, dappled sunlight or shade. Needs shelter from strong wind.

Soil   Needs soil to be enriched with organic matter well ahead of planting.

Support   Staking is necessary unless foxgloves are planted in a very protected position.

GROWING METHOD

Planting   Sow the very small seed in trays or pots, barely covered. Sow in late summer and plant out or pot up singly when large enough to handle. Space 16 in apart.

Watering   Give regular deep watering, especially in dry, windy conditions. Mulching helps to retain soil moisture.

Fertilizing   Complete plant food may be applied monthly throughout spring and summer but fertilizing is not essential.

Problems   No special problems.

FLOWERING

Season   Spring and summer. In cool zones they may flower summer into autumn.

Cutting   Not particularly good as a cut flower.

AFTER FLOWERING

General   Once stems have flowered, cut them off just above the leaves. Plants may then produce several shorter flowering stems, especially in cool areas. Discard plants after the second flowering flush.

GLOBE AMARANTH

Gomphrena globosa

SOMETIMES CALLED bachelor's buttons, globe amaranths are among the best annuals for growing in hot climates.

LOW GROWING and long flowering, globe amaranths are used in this garden as an edging to massed agapanthus.

FEATURES

Also known as bachelor's buttons, the globe amaranth is a tall shrubby plant with hairy leaves that grows to 12–18 in. It usually has rounded heads of magenta-purple flowers, although pink, white and mauve strains are sometimes available. A dwarf form with yellow-orange flowers is known as 'Little Buddy.' These plants are best used in massed plantings or in borders.

CONDITIONS

Climate   Not suitable for very cold areas.
Aspect   Must have a sunny spot.
Soil   Needs well-drained soil enriched with manure or compost.

GROWING METHOD

Planting   Sow in spring in pots or trays. Transplant seedlings out 10–12 in apart when they are large enough to handle.

Watering   Once plants are established, a good weekly soaking should be enough to maintain the growth and display.
Fertilizing   Apply liquid or granular fertilizer monthly once plants are 4–6 in high.
Problems   No special problems.

FLOWERING

Season   Summer and autumn.
Cutting   Can be used as a cut flower. Flowers can also be dried by hanging them upside down in a dry, airy place for use in dried arrangements.

AFTER FLOWERING

General   Remove plants after they have finished flowering and discard them.

GODETIA
Clarkia amoena

THIS DISPLAY *shows just some of the range of colors available. Godetias are first rate cut flowers, lasting a week in water.*

IN EUROPE *godetia is called "farewell to spring," because it is the last of the spring annuals to come into bloom.*

FEATURES

Also known as farewell to spring and rocky mountain garland, godetia bridges the gap between spring and summer displays as it flowers much later than many spring blooming annuals. It grows 12–30 in tall on thin, upright stems with pointed leaves. The cup-shaped flowers come in red, white, pink and lavender. They have a distinctive satiny appearance. Attractive when mass planted.

CONDITIONS

Climate   Does well in cool to warm areas. Not suitable for tropical regions.

Aspect   Needs an open, sunny position.

Soil   Does not need rich soil but does require perfect drainage.

GROWING METHOD

Planting   Sow where plants are to grow or in pots during autumn. Barely cover seed. Transplant seedlings 8–12 in apart.

Watering   Once plants are established, water heavily only when soil has begun to dry out. Overwatering kills plants.

Fertilizing   Not generally necessary, but some bone meal or complete plant food could be applied when plants are well established.

Problems   No special problems but overwatering causes root rot and death of plants.

FLOWERING

Season   Middle to late spring, continuing into early summer in cooler areas.

Cutting   Excellent cut flower.

AFTER FLOWERING

General   Remove the plants once they start to look untidy.

HOLLYHOCK
Alcea rosea

HOLLYHOCK MIXTURES usually come in harmonious tones, as is certainly the case here, but straight colors are also available.

LORDING IT over a mixed planting, hollyhocks do tend to lean—if you don't like the effect, give each a short stake.

FEATURES

An essential element of cottage gardens, this biennial may be grown as an annual. Tall forms grow to 8 ft, a shorter variety to 3 ft. Single and double flowers occur in most colors except blue. Plants are best planted in groups at the back of a border, or behind or between smaller shrubs.

CONDITIONS

Climate   Can be grown in cool or warm areas. Not suitable for tropical regions.
Aspect   Needs sun and a sheltered position.
Soil   Prepare soil with generous applications of manure or compost as plants are heavy feeders. Must have good drainage.
Support   Should be self-supporting if well grown and protected from strong wind.

GROWING METHOD

Planting In warm areas sow seed in early spring where it is to grow or in pots. In cooler areas sow in late summer in pots and plant out the following spring.

Watering   Once they are planted out, give seedlings deep regular waterings so that they will develop the substantial root system necessary to support such a tall plant. Frequent shallow watering is inadvisable: it causes surface rooting and weak plants are liable to fall over.
Fertilizing If soil has been well prepared, a monthly application of complete plant food should be all that is required.
Problems   Prone to rust, a fungal disease that is unsightly and ultimately weakens growth. Spraying with copper oxychloride or Zineb may be necessary if the attack is severe.

FLOWERING

Season   Spring sown seedlings grow rapidly and flower in late summer and autumn. Cool zone sowings made in late summer flower the following summer.
Cutting Not suitable for cutting; best left for display in the garden.

AFTER FLOWERING

General Remove individual dead flowers during the flowering season. Once flowering has ceased, remove the plants.

HONESTY
Lunaria annua

THE SEED PODS may be the chief attraction, but honesty also has a beautiful display of flowers. They last well when cut.

MAUVE FLOWERS are the most common. Here they grow with a variegated white variety. There is a variegated mauve one, too.

FEATURES

Honesty is also known as money plant and is usually grown for its circular, smooth, silvery seed "pods" that, with a bit of imagination, can be thought to resemble coins. It grows to 18–28 in, with toothed leaves and rosy or mauve flowers. The silvery seed pods are decorative in the house or garden.

CONDITIONS

Climate   Prefers cool climates but can be grown in warm areas.

Aspect   Prefers half a day's sun or dappled shade.

Soil   Needs no special soil preparation but you can add a dressing of lime, 3½ oz per square yard, to very acid soils.

GROWING METHOD

Planting   Sow in autumn or spring in pots or directly into the ground. Space the seeds approximately 12 in apart.

Watering   Tolerates occasional drying out. Give regular deep watering throughout the warmer months.

Fertilizing   Needs little fertilizer. If desired, give complete plant food once seedlings are established and again when flower buds are forming.

FLOWERING

Season   From the middle of spring into summer, especially in cooler areas.

Cutting   May be used as a cut flower but most people prefer to leave the flowers to mature on the plant.

AFTER FLOWERING

General   Flowers left to mature and die on the plant produce the silvery seed "pods" greatly sought after for dried arrangements. Cut when pods are mature and dry. Hang upside down in a dry, airy place until you can carefully remove the outer skin of the pod. Remove spent plants—you will find plenty of seedlings coming up next year.

JOHNNY-JUMP-UP

Viola tricolor

JOHNNY-JUMP-UPS take their name from the way they come up from self-sown seed, often in various patterns and colors as here.

TRI-COLORED FLOWERS in distinctive purple, white and gold are the most common variety of johnny-jump-up.

FEATURES

Also known as heartsease, johnny-jump-up is compact when young, sprawling as it ages. It grows 6–10 in tall. The small, pansy flowers have delightful "kitten" faces in two tones of violet and yellow. Use it in mass plantings, as a filler or border edging, or in pots or troughs.

CONDITIONS

Climate   Grows well in all cool to warm areas.
Aspect   Tolerates full sun or half shade.
Soil   Tolerates most soil conditions but grows especially vigorously if the soil has a high organic content.

GROWING METHOD

Planting   In warm zones sow in late summer to autumn; in cool zones early spring sowings are best. Sow directly into the ground or in pots. Barely cover seed. Plant out when seedlings are manageable at 6–8 in spacings.

Watering   Once plants are established, a heavy weekly watering should be sufficient unless weather is very windy and dry.
Fertilizing   Should not need supplementary fertilizer, especially if soil has been enriched with compost or manure.
Problems   No special problems.

FLOWERING

Season   Spring in warm zones, late summer in cool zones where seed was sown during early spring. Regular dead-heading extends flowering time.
Cutting   Flower stems are short but flowers look lovely in small bouquets.

AFTER FLOWERING

General   When plants become lanky and untidy, pull them out and discard them. They will probably have self-seeded and so you can expect seedlings the following year.

KALE
Brassica oleracea acephala

KALE IS IDEAL for giving color in rainy winter climates—even a downpour that would batter a bed of flowers leaves them undamaged. The frilly or plain leaves are brilliantly colored and more than make up for the disappointing small yellow flowers.

FEATURES

Also known as ornamental or flowering kale, kale is a small, frilled cabbage grown for its colorful foliage. Usually less than 12 in high, it is suitable for garden display or pots. The leaves show brilliant colors of red, purple, pink and white in streaks and blotches on the green.

CONDITIONS

Climate   Can be grown in cool or warm areas. Not suitable for tropical regions.
Aspect   Needs full sun for best color.
Soil   Enrich soil with decayed compost or manure ahead of planting and apply 3 1/2 oz of lime per square yard.

GROWING METHOD

Planting   Sow in late summer or early autumn in pots as the seed is fine; barely cover it. Plant out into the ground or individual pots when seedlings are 1–2 in high. In the ground, space at 12 in intervals.

Watering   Needs regular deep watering to promote large, well-formed plants. Allow any potted specimens to dry out a little between watering.
Fertilizing   Give a monthly application of granular or liquid fertilizer once plants are established.
Problems   Like all members of the cabbage family, kale is very attractive to snails, slugs and caterpillars. Check regularly to remove pests and search for culprits at night, if necessary, with a flashlight.

FLOWERING

Season   Not grown for its flowers—pinch out any precocious flower buds. Plants are normally at their best in late winter and spring.
Cutting   The whole head would have to be cut but kale makes a striking, unusual decoration.

AFTER FLOWERING

General   Once flowers appear, plants are usually past their peak and they should then be dug up and discarded.

LADIES' PURSES

Calceolaria herbeohybrida

POUCH-SHAPED FLOWERS, which are much more attractive than they sound, cover these lovely plants. They give it its common name.

LADIES' PURSES are rarely a straight color—even this one, which at first sight looks plain orange, is veined and shaded with scarlet.

FEATURES

Also known as slipper flower, ladies' purses is a popular pot plant for indoor use. It cannot be grown successfully in the garden. It grows to 6–12 in with oval, hairy leaves. Pouched flowers in bright red, yellow, orange, tan or cream come in plain colors or in spotted or blotched varieties.

CONDITIONS

Climate	Suitable for cool and warm zones only. Will not tolerate extremes of heat or cold.
Aspect	Not suitable for outdoor display. Keep in bright, indirect light, away from windows.
Soil	Must have well-drained potting mix.

GROWING METHOD

Planting	Difficult to start from seed without ideal nursery conditions. Lightly scatter very fine seed on the surface of the seed-starting mix and leave the seed uncovered. Pot up seedlings singly when they are 1–2 in high. Many people find it easier to buy a potted plant in bud or flower.

Watering	Water regularly but never let the potting mix become soggy. Don't allow water to remain in the saucers for longer than about half an hour after watering.
Fertilizing	Apply liquid fertilizer once plants are established in individual pots and then apply a weak solution once a week.
Problems	No special problems but overwatering causes rotting and death of plants.

FLOWERING

Season	Late winter and spring.
Cutting	Not suitable for cutting.

AFTER FLOWERING

General	Discard these plants after they have finished their flowering.

LARKSPUR

Consolida ambigua

RED AND WHITE spikes of larkspur make a brilliant display in this garden. They closely resemble delphiniums but are not so tall.

HIGHLY DISSECTED LEAVES are the distinguishing feature of larkspur. Despite a tendency to lean, they rarely need staking.

FEATURES

Also known as sweet rocket, larkspurs are related to delphiniums but are not as tall. They are a must for a traditional cottage garden, and make a lovely garden display when planted in drifts or as a background to smaller annuals. Larkspur grows to 20–28 in and has tall spikes of pink, white, red and violet flowers, with finely cut leaves.

CONDITIONS

Climate Can be grown in cool or warm areas. Not suitable for tropical regions.

Aspect Needs full sun with some form of protection from wind.

Soil Soil needs to be enriched with manure or compost well ahead of planting. Soil must be well drained.

Support Plants should support each other and not need artificial support.

GROWING METHOD

Planting Sow direct where the plants are to grow for best results. In warm zones sow in autumn, in cool zones in spring. Space about 6 in apart for massed effect.

Watering Regular, deep watering is essential. Mulch to conserve moisture as they don't like to dry out completely, but they don't like to be waterlogged either.

Fertilizing Apply complete plant food monthly after plants are growing strongly.

Problems Leaf spotting and rots can occur in very wet conditions. Watch for aphids.

FLOWERING

Season In warm zones middle to late spring; in cool zones summer.

Cutting Excellent cut flower. Cut long stems and scald ends before soaking in cool water.

AFTER FLOWERING

General Dig out the plants once they have finished flowering and are past their prime.

LINARIA
Linaria maroccana

EACH LINARIA FLOWER is like a tiny snapdragon, and in the United States it is sometimes called "baby snapdragon." The flowers have a touch of yellow on the lower lip, and from a slight distance the effect is softly toned yet scintillating. Best when planted en masse, it can also be used in rockeries.

FEATURES

Linaria is also known as toad flax and as eggs and bacon. It has dainty little flowers like tiny snapdragons—they come in a wide color range including white, cream, yellow and red. Linaria grows to 12–18 in and is ideal for massed planting or planting in drifts. It can also be grown to fill spaces in front of shrubs or in pockets of a rock garden. Perennial forms of linaria are also available. They include *L. genistifolia*, with orange-marked flowers, and the blue-flowered *L. purpurea*.

CONDITIONS

Climate Can be grown well in cool and warm areas. Not suitable for tropical regions.

Aspect Prefers full sun but tolerates half a day's sun.

Soil Needs well-drained soil enriched with manure or compost ahead of planting.

GROWING METHOD

Planting Seeds are best sown where they are to grow. In warm zones sow in autumn, in cool zones in spring. Space 2 in apart.

Watering Give regular deep watering to establish. Tolerates drying out between watering once plants are fairly mature. Use a gentle spray so as not to flatten plants.

Fertilizing Apply complete plant food once a month until buds form.

Problems No special problems.

FLOWERING

Season Spring in warm areas, summer in cool zones.

Cutting Can be used as a cut flower if picked when flowers are fully out but not faded.

AFTER FLOWERING

General Cut back hard as you may get a second flush of flowers. When plants look untidy or past their peak, dig them out and discard.

LIVINGSTONE DAISY

Dorotheanthus bellidiformis

NOT TRULY A DAISY but a member of the mesembryanthemum family, the Livingstone daisy closes its flowers in shade—which is why they should get as much sunshine as possible. The name Dorotheanthus, *"Dorothy's flower," was a tribute from a German botanist to his mother.*

FEATURES

Livingstone daisy is a good plant for seaside gardens and is ideal for mass planting on banks, in rockeries, in pots and hanging baskets. It has a prostrate habit, spreading to 16–20 in, but is only 4–6 in high. It has fleshy leaves with very bright, daisy-type flowers in shades of red, pink, orange, white, mauve and cream.

CONDITIONS

Climate Not suitable for cold areas.

Aspect Needs full sun all day.

Soil Needs perfectly drained soil. No special soil preparation needed as plants seem to prefer poor soil as long as drainage is good.

GROWING METHOD

Planting Sow seed in late summer to autumn, directly into the ground or into pots. In cool zones sow seed under cover and delay transplanting seedlings until spring. Barely cover the seed. Space the seeds about 6 in apart in their permanent positions.

Watering

Watering Water regularly to establish but once established keep fairly dry throughout the growing season. Overwatering quickly kills these plants.

Fertilizing Not necessary, although a light dressing of bone meal or pelleted poultry manure may be given when plants are well established in the ground.

Problems No special problems but overwet conditions cause rapid rotting and death of plants.

FLOWERING

Season From late winter to spring in tropical zones, into early summer in warm zones; usually summer in cool zones. Flowers close on dull, cloudy days.

Cutting Not suitable for cutting.

AFTER FLOWERING

General Dig out plants once they are past their peak.

LOBELIA

Lobelia erinus

LOBELIA FLOWERS may be small, but they specialize in lovely vivid blues and they bloom in large numbers over a long season.

IN THIS HANGING BASKET, lobelias contrast most effectively with begonias. They look more purple than they are.

FEATURES

This ideal edging plant, filler, pot or basket subject has neat, mounded growth to about 4–6 in. It makes a lovely splash of color in the garden, with its mostly blue flowers. They range in color from deep royal blue to sky blue. Mixtures containing blue with white eye, magenta, mauve and white, as well as plain blue, are also available.

CONDITIONS

Climate   Grows well in cool and warm zones. Not suitable for tropical areas.

Aspect   Tolerates half shade but flowers best when grown in full sun.

Soil   Enrich soil with compost or manure before planting. Drainage must be good.

GROWING METHOD

Planting   In warm zones sow in autumn, in cool zones in spring. Barely cover the tiny seed. Space the seed 4–6 in apart in its permanent positions. Close plant pots and baskets for a full effect.

Watering   Water regularly and thoroughly to maintain plants through their fairly long season.

Fertilizing   Monthly applications of complete plant food will be beneficial once the plants are growing strongly.

Problems   Mottling of leaves may be caused by earth mites. Keep area weed free and promptly remove affected plants. There are no other special problems.

FLOWERING

Season   Later winter through spring, and sometimes into early summer. Flowering is a little later in cool zones.

Cutting   Not suitable for cutting.

AFTER FLOWERING

General   Plants can be cut back after first flowering, which may induce a second flush. An application of liquid plant food after cutting back should promote good growth. If plants respond, continue monthly fertilizing. Pull the plants out when they are past their peak. Sometimes they self-seed and seedlings appear the following season.

LOVE-IN-A-MIST

Nigella damascena

'MISS JEKYLL,' has double, clear blue flowers. It is the best known variety of love-in-a-mist.

AFTER THE FLOWERS come the curiously attractive seed vessels that give the plant its alternative name, devil-in-a-bush.

FEATURES

Also known as devil-in-a-bush, love-in-a-mist has fine, feathery foliage, with a fringe of the foliage surrounding and slightly veiling the flower. This gives the flower its common names. Flowers are mostly blue but pale and deep pink, white and purple varieties also occur. Love-in-a-mist grows 16–24 in high and is good for mass planting in beds or as a filler between shrubs.

CONDITIONS

Climate Suitable for all warm to cool areas.
Aspect Does well in full sun but does tolerate half a day's sun.
Soil Needs good drainage but isn't too fussy about soils. Organic matter may be dug in ahead of time, but this is not essential.

GROWING METHOD

Planting Sow in autumn or early spring. Space plants at intervals of about 6–8 in.
Watering Once plants are established a deep soaking once a week should be enough.
Fertilizing Does not need supplementary fertilizer, although a monthly liquid feed may increase flower size.

Problems No special problems.

FLOWERING

Season Spring and early summer.
Cutting Delightful cut flower. Remove foliage from lower part of stalk to prolong flower life.

AFTER FLOWERING

General The inflated seed pods that form are useful in dried arrangements. Pick stems after pods have dried on plant and hang upside down in an airy place. Plants can then be pulled out. They self-seed prolifically— you will have more than enough for the following season.

HINT

Seeds Seeds of this plant are very aromatic and have been used as a spice to flavor cakes, breads and curries. In India, seeds of this and another related species are used as a moth repellent.

LUPIN

Lupinus hartwegii

ANNUAL LUPINS rarely come in straight colors, but the mixtures of soft, cool tones in white, pink and blue are always harmonious and pretty. They make a lovely massed display but they also look most attractive when planted with a mixture of other annuals or among perennials.

FEATURES

Lupins are fine plants for general garden display, especially where soft colors are desired. They grow to 12–18 in with divided, hairy leaves and pea-shaped blue, white or pink flowers. Other species of annual lupins are the yellow-flowered *L. luteus* and the Texas bluebonnet, *L. texensis*.

CONDITIONS

Climate   Grows well in all cool to warm areas.
Aspect   Needs full sun.
Soil   Needs well-drained soil that has been lightly limed before planting. Soil need not be especially rich.

GROWING METHOD

Planting   Best sown where they are to grow, placed 8–12 in apart. Sow in autumn into moist soil. Water in well and do not water again until seedlings appear, unless the weather is very dry and windy.

Watering   Once plants are established and growing strongly, water deeply about once a week.
Fertilizing   Should need very little fertilizer as lupins fix nitrogen in nodules on their roots. A low nitrogen fertilizer could be applied when buds first appear.
Problems   Earth mites and a virus disease may occasionally cause problems. Remove any plants that look unhealthy.

FLOWERING

Season   Late winter and early spring; late spring in cool areas.
Cutting   Good cut flower if picked when buds are showing color. Scald stems to prolong life.

AFTER FLOWERING

General   Remove spent flowers throughout the growing season. When flowering is finished, dig plants in or add them to compost.

MADAGASCAR PERIWINKLE

Catharanthus roseus

NOT ONLY PRETTY, the Madagascar periwinkle is also useful. It is a source of drugs used in treating some forms of cancer.

SEEDS USUALLY COME in mixed colors, but the white variety is sometimes offered separately. It is especially lovely grown in shade.

FEATURES

Somewhat succulent stems with pink/rose, mauve or white flowers are characteristic of the Madagascar periwinkle. The flowers have a deeper center. Madagascar periwinkle is a spreading plant that grows to 8–12 in. It is suitable for massed garden display and can also be grown in pots.

CONDITIONS

Climate	Can be grown in any warm zone or in any tropical area.
Aspect	Tolerates full sun or semi-shade.
Soil	Needs good drainage but enrich the soil with manure or compost ahead of planting.

GROWING METHOD

Planting	Sow seed in late winter to early spring—this plant dislikes cold weather. Lightly cover the seed and keep the mix just moist until seedlings appear. Space seedlings out about 8–12 in apart in their final positions, either in the garden or in containers, once they are large enough to handle.

Watering	Needs regular deep watering for prolonged display, but take care not to overwater as plants will rot.
Fertilizing	Apply granular or liquid complete plant food monthly to keep plants growing vigorously throughout both the growing period and the flowering period.
Problems	No special problems except that poor drainage and overwet soils cause rotting and rapid death of plants.

FLOWERING

Season	Throughout summer and earlier in tropical areas.
Cutting	Not suitable for cutting.

AFTER FLOWERING

General	Remove plants once they have finished flowering and are past their peak.

MARIGOLD
Tagetes

SINGLE FRENCH MARIGOLDS combine daintiness with a bright and unusual color range: yellows, oranges and mahogany reds.

'PETITE YELLOW,' a French marigold, is a scaled-down version of a big African one. They all come from Mexico, not France or Africa.

FEATURES

Ease of growing and long flowering are the hallmarks of marigolds. Upright growth reaches 30–40 in for African marigolds (*T. erecta*) and 8–16 in for French marigolds (*T. patula*). They have strong-smelling, divided leaves and rounded or flattened flowers in yellows and oranges (African), or orange, yellow, mahogany and crimson (French). They are suitable for massed plantings and pots.

CONDITIONS

Climate   Can be grown in all but the coldest climates.
Aspect   Must have a well-drained, sunny position. African marigolds need wind protection.
Soil   Not fussy about soils.

GROWING METHOD

Planting   Sow African marigolds in warm zones in early to mid-spring; in cool zones sow them in late spring. Sow French marigolds in late summer or early autumn in warm zones, and in early summer in cool zones. Sow both varieties directly into the ground or in pots. Space plants about 8–16 in apart, depending on the variety.

Watering   Give regular, deep watering, especially during dry, windy weather. Mulching between plants helps conserve soil moisture.
Fertilizing   Apply complete granular or liquid plant food monthly, once plants are well established, so that they are sustained throughout their long growing period.
Problems   Sometimes plants are attacked by mites and whiteflies. You can try hosing them off. Leaves may be attacked by leaf miners but it is probably best to ignore them as they can only be controlled by the use of very strong systemic pesticides.

FLOWERING

Season   Depends on sowing time. Mostly through summer and autumn. May flower into winter in warm areas.
Cutting   Good cut flowers, long lasting with frequent water changes. Some people find their smell quite unpleasant.

AFTER FLOWERING

General   Remove plants once they are past the stage of their best flowering.

MEADOWFOAM

Limnanthes douglasii

MEADOWFOAM is sometimes called the poached egg flower for its combination of white and bright yellow.

A LOVELY EFFECT of massed flowers tumbling down the slope: meadowfoam is here planted on either side of a flight of steps.

FEATURES

Meadowfoam has slightly cupped white flowers with bright yellow centers, a distinctive appearance that explains its alternative common names of poached egg flower and fried eggs. These plants are excellent for edgings, damp rockeries and for planting between pavers as they like a cool, damp root run. They grow to about 8–12 in high.

CONDITIONS

Climate   Grows well in warm or cool zones. Not suitable for very cold or tropical areas.
Aspect   Prefers full sun.
Soil   Needs a moisture-retentive soil. Dig organic matter into the soil well ahead of planting to aid moisture retention.

GROWING METHOD

Planting   Sow in autumn or very early spring where they are to grow. Cover lightly and keep just moist. Space 6–8 in apart.
Watering   Keep soil just slightly damp, but not soggy, at all times.
Fertilizing Don't overfertilize. Apply one application only of complete plant food when plants have been well established.
Problems   No special problems.

FLOWERING

Season   Spring into early summer.
Cutting   Not suitable for cutting.

AFTER FLOWERING

General   Remove plants once they start to look leggy and untidy.

MEXICAN SUNFLOWER
Tithonia rotundifolia

THE MEXICAN SUNFLOWER does indeed come from Mexico. The flowers are large—about 6 in across.

LUMINOUS without being harsh or gaudy, the Mexican sunflowers are an especially lovely shade of orange.

FEATURES

A reliable, easy-care annual, Mexican sunflower has very deep orange, daisy-like flowers. It is a tall, spreading plant that grows to over 3 ft high. Because of its height, it is best planted at the back of borders or in massed plantings. This useful and colorful annual is also very drought tolerant.

CONDITIONS

Climate   Suitable for warm or tropical areas only.
Aspect   Must have full sun, and it also needs some wind protection.
Soil   Not fussy about soils but needs good drainage. No special preparation needed.
Support   Support is generally not needed despite plants being so tall.

GROWING METHOD

Planting   Sow directly into the ground or into pots in spring. Space at least 20 in apart.

Watering   Once plants are established, they tolerate long dry periods. Water heavily when necessary but probably not more often than every ten days.
Fertilizing   Probably not necessary but one application of complete plant food could be applied when plants are growing strongly.
Problems   No particular problems.

FLOWERING

Season   Throughout summer, especially if spent blooms are removed regularly.
Cutting   Suitable for use as a cut flower.

AFTER FLOWERING

General   Remove plants after flowering. They may self-seed so that seedlings come up next year.

HINT

Uses   For a bright splash of "hot" garden colors, use Mexican sunflower with bright yellow and orange cosmos 'Bright Lights,' yellow calliopsis and red salvia.

MIGNONETTE
Reseda odorata

GREEN MIGNONETTE flowers are so inconspicuous the flowers could pass unnoticed if it wasn't for their perfume.

A BIT LESS SWEET than the green variety, the red and yellow ones do, however, make much more of a splash in the garden.

FEATURES

A very sweet perfume is a feature of mignonette, which grows 8–12 in high in a rounded shape. Old-fashioned mignonette has greenish and pinky-red flowers; other varieties have yellow, red or coppery flowers. Plant in pots or among other flowers in spots where their fragrance will be appreciated.

CONDITIONS

Climate   Suitable for growing in warm or cool climates.
Aspect   Prefers full sun but tolerates semi-shade.
Soil   Needs well-drained soil. Dig in organic matter ahead of planting time and add lime to soil, 3½ oz per square yard, before planting.

GROWING METHOD

Planting   Sow in autumn in warm areas and in spring in cooler zones. Sow directly into permanent positions, spaced about 8 in apart.

Watering   Give regular deep watering throughout the growing season but take care that the soil does not become soggy.
Fertilizing   With good soil preparation little feeding should be needed, but complete plant food could be applied once or twice during the growing season.
Problems   No particular problems.

FLOWERING

Season   Late winter to early spring in warm zones, summer in cool areas. More flowers are produced if the growing tips of young plants are pinched out to promote branching.
Cutting   Widely used as a cut flower because of its fragrance. Can be used alone or mixed with more colorful flowers.

AFTER FLOWERING

General   Remove plants once flowering is finished.

MONKEY FLOWER
Mimulus

MIMULUS MEANS "a little actor" and the colors and patterns of these flowers do almost look like stage make-up.

MONKEY FLOWERS are among the few brightly colored annuals that like a bit of shade, but they don't like drought.

FEATURES

Good for cool, damp places in gardens, monkey flowers also do well in pots. Some species are perennial but in temperate areas they are best treated as annuals. There is a wide range of heights from 8 in to 3 ft. Most flowers are in the red and yellow color range, many with spotted flowers.

CONDITIONS

Climate Not suitable for the tropics or hot dry areas. Best in cool areas.
Aspect Needs semi-shade.
Soil Needs moist soil. Dig in plenty of rotted organic matter well ahead of planting to retain the moisture.

GROWING METHOD

Planting Sow the extremely fine seed indoors in late winter, in pots or trays. Barely cover it and keep it just moist. Plant out at 6–8 in intervals in spring.

Watering Never let plants be short of water throughout their growing season but do not leave water in the saucers of pot-grown plants.
Fertilizing Monthly applications of complete plant food may be given once plants are well established, but this is not essential.
Problems No particular problems.

FLOWERING

Season Spring and summer.
Cutting Not suitable for cutting.

AFTER FLOWERING

General Discard plants once flowering finishes.

HINT

Planting These cheerful flowers can be planted in damp soil around the edges of ornamental pools if they are shaded by taller plants.

MOON FLOWER

Ipomoea alba

MOONFLOWERS open amazingly fast at sunset, to gleam in the fading light, but by the middle of the next morning they have withered. Each fragrant "moon" is embossed with a star: white on white on the front, lime green on the back.

FEATURES

A climbing plant with large, fragrant satiny white flowers that open at night, moon flower grows as an annual in most areas but in very warm areas is perennial. In some tropical areas it has become a "weedy" garden escaper. It grows 6–9 ft high and can become rampant in warm, humid climates. Grow it either in the ground or in a tub with support.

CONDITIONS

Climate Suitable for warm and tropical areas only.
Aspect Tolerates sun or semi-shade.
Soil Tolerates wide range of soil conditions. If soil is enriched with organic matter the plant should grow very fast.
Support A twining climber, it needs wire or trellis on which to climb.

GROWING METHOD

Planting Seed has a very hard coat that needs nicking or filing to allow water to penetrate, but don't be too vigorous and go too far. Sow seed where it is to grow in late winter or spring. If planting more than one seed, space them out at least 3 ft apart.

Watering Once plants are established, a heavy weekly watering should be sufficient. Pot-grown specimens may need more frequent watering.
Fertilizing Little or no supplementary fertilizer should be needed. Give pot-grown plants slow release fertilizer or biweekly applications of a liquid fertilizer.
Problems No particular problems.

FLOWERING

Season Summer.
Cutting Unsuitable for cutting.

AFTER FLOWERING

General Remove plants when they die down or when foliage starts to go yellow. However, you may like to leave them if you have space to see whether they grow again next year.

NASTURTIUM

Tropaeolum majus

SELF-SOWN NASTURTIUMS *tend to revert to this old-fashioned orange type, but they are no less welcome for that.*

LUXURIANT FOLIAGE *and bright flowers belie the nasturtium's forgiveness of drought and poor soil. They are as easy as can be to grow.*

FEATURES

Nasturtium is a good choice for children to plant as the seeds are large and easy to handle and grow. The leaves and flowers are also edible. It forms a low bush or trailing plant 8–12 in high, and trailing plants may extend almost a yard. It has bright green, rounded leaves and bright flowers in red, yellow, orange, cream or crimson. Use nasturtiums for informal garden display, groundcovers or troughs. It also makes a great effect in a hanging basket.

CONDITIONS

Climate	Suitable for tropical to cool areas.
Aspect	Needs full sun.
Soil	Needs good drainage. Does not need rich soil and so no special preparation.

GROWING METHOD

Planting	Best sown in early spring where they are to grow. Sow singly or in clumps at 8–20 in intervals, depending on variety. In cool areas sow in late spring to early summer.

Watering	Once plants are established, water heavily every seven to ten days. Don't overwater.
Fertilizing	Should not need supplementary fertilizer. Over-rich soil and fertilizer promotes leaf growth at the expense of flowers.
Problems	No particular problems.

FLOWERING

Season	Late spring through summer; later in cooler areas. May flower into autumn too.
Cutting	Good cut flower and frequent picking helps promote a longer flowering period.

AFTER FLOWERING

General	Often self-seeds—you may find plants coming up under the old ones. When plants look too untidy, pull them out.

NEMESIA

Nemesia strumosa

NEMESIAS COME in every bright color, from white and yellow to orange and red. There is a clear blue, smaller flowered variety, too.

THEIR SEASON BEING SHORT, nemesias are best planted with other flowers, such as the stocks and love-in-a-mist used here.

FEATURES

This very colorful plant grows 12–16 in high; dwarf strains grow to 8 in. Flowers come in a wide color range, including yellow, white, purple and blue, and provide an eye catching display, especially when used in massed plantings. It is also effective if it is close planted in tubs or troughs.

CONDITIONS

Climate   Can be grown in warm and cool areas. Not suitable for tropical regions.
Aspect   Does best in an open, sunny spot.
Soil   Enrich soil with organic matter well ahead of planting time. Drainage must be good.

GROWING METHOD

Planting   In warm zones sow in late summer to early autumn, in cool zones in spring. Sow directly into the ground or into pots, lightly covering the fine seed. When seedlings are large enough to handle, plant them out at intervals of 6–8 in.

Watering   Once plant is established, a deep weekly soaking should be sufficient unless the weather is very dry and windy.
Fertilizing   Apply complete plant food once a month until buds appear.
Problems   No particular problems.

FLOWERING

Season   In warm zones in later winter to spring, in cool zones in summer. To promote more flower heads, pinch out growing tips of plants when they are 3–4 in high.
Cutting   May be used as a cut flower but best kept for garden display.

AFTER FLOWERING

General   Cut back spent blooms to encourage flowering from the lower stems. Once all flowering is finished, dig the plants out.

PAINTED TONGUE

Salpiglossis sinuata

EACH TRUMPET-SHAPED flower displays an intricate embroidery of golden veins over a rich ground color.

MIXES OF RICH COLORS such as these are what you can expect if you buy a packet of mixed seed. Single colors are not usually sold.

FEATURES

These brilliantly colored flowers grow to 24–36 in on tall stems with light green foliage. The blooms are trumpet shaped and come in a variety of colors, with distinctive patterned veins and markings. Painted tongue should be mass planted to display the wide color range.

CONDITIONS

Climate　Difficult to grow in very cold areas. Best in warm to cool areas.

Aspect　Must have full sun and some protection from the wind.

Soil　Drainage must be good or plants rot. Prepare soil well ahead of planting by digging in plenty of manure or compost.

Support　Close planting should ensure that plants are self-supporting.

GROWING METHOD

Planting　Sow seed in spring directly where they are to grow or into pots. Cover the fine seed very lightly. Plant out the seedlings at 8 in spacings once they are large enough to handle. Pinching out the growing tips when the plants are 3–4 in high will encourage them to branch.

Watering　Once plants are established, water heavily only every week or so unless conditions are very hot and windy, when you will need to water more frequently. This is far better than frequent light sprinklings.

Fertilizing　If soil has been well prepared, little additional fertilizer should be needed. If desired, bone meal or pelleted poultry manure may be applied when seedlings are well established in the ground, and then again when the first buds have appeared.

Problems　No special problems but overwatering or poor drainage can cause root rots and the eventual death of plants.

FLOWERING

Season　A long display throughout summer if spent flowers are regularly removed.

Cutting　May be used as a cut flower but is best left for the spectacular garden display.

AFTER FLOWERING

General　Dig out plants once they begin to look untidy as they will not improve.

PANSY
Viola x *wittrockiana*

NOT ALL PANSIES feature the traditional black and maroon blotches. This one in two shades of blue is called "Bingo."

THIS IS "THE JOKER." The patterns of colors and lines radiating from the center of the flower guide pollinating insects to the nectar.

FEATURES

Lovely whether grown in pots and troughs or as mass plantings, pansies have never gone out of fashion. Lightly scented in a huge range of colors, the flowers have darker centers so that they resemble little "faces." They grow only 6–10 in high but the clumps can spread up to 10–12 in across.

CONDITIONS

Climate Can be grown in any cool or warm area.
Aspect Tolerates full sun or semi-shade.
Soil Enrich soil with plenty of compost or manure ahead of planting time. Drainage for pansies must be good.

GROWING METHOD

Planting Sow in autumn in warm zones or in spring in cool zones. The fine seed is best sown lightly covered in pots or trays and planted out at about 6 in intervals when seedlings are 1–2 in high.

Watering Needs deep regular watering to promote strong growth and good flowering. Once a week should be enough unless weather is very dry and windy.
Fertilizing Apply liquid plant food at biweekly intervals once plants are growing strongly.
Problems No special problems but poor drainage or overwatering kills plants.

FLOWERING

Season In warm zones in late winter and spring, in cool zones in summer. Maintain the long blooming period with regular removal of the spent flowers.
Cutting Very good cut flower. Arrange in float bowls or add to small bouquets.

AFTER FLOWERING

Problems Dig out plants once they begin to look lanky and untidy.

PAPER DAISY

Helichrysum

THE LIGHT-REFLECTING surface of the flowers gives their already bright colors added brilliance in the garden.

PAPER DAISY plants are apt to be rather leggy and boring in leaf, but the range of flower colors can be stunning, as shown here.

FEATURES

Also known as starflowers, paper daisies may grow from 8 in to nearly 3 ft high. They have slightly woolly gray to green leaves and the flowers can be bright golden yellow, sometimes touched with brown, or they can be bronze, red or cream.

CONDITIONS

Climate   Difficult to grow in very humid climates; does best in warm to cool areas.

Aspect   Must have full sun.

Soil   Needs very well-drained, light and friable soil.

GROWING METHOD

Planting   Sow seed where it is to grow or in pots. Sow in late autumn or winter; in cool areas sow in spring. Lightly cover the fine seed and water carefully so as not to dislodge it. When the seedlings are large enough to handle, plant them out at intervals of about 8 in. Cultivars can be grown from cuttings of young growth.

Watering   Water regularly until plants are established, and then water heavily every seven to ten days. Allow the soil to dry out between waterings.

Fertilizing   Generally not necessary. Any fertilizer used should contain little or no phosphorus.

Problems   Poor drainage or overwatering kills plants. In showery, humid weather, plants may collapse. Watch out for leaf-eating caterpillars, which can be troublesome.

FLOWERING

Season   Long flowering through spring and summer, sometimes into autumn. Regular removal of spent flowers helps prolong flowering.

Cutting   Ideal cut flower that dries and lasts for years. Pick the flowers when the petals are well formed but still incurved. Hang the bunches upside down in a dry, airy place to complete the drying process.

AFTER FLOWERING

General   Dig plants out and discard them when flowering has finished.

PETUNIA

Petunia hybrida

THE COLOR RANGE is enormous: everything but orange. Strains with deeper veining on a lighter ground are especially handsome.

WHITE PETUNIAS always look cool and fresh, whether on their own or associated with other petunias. They are subtly scented.

FEATURES

Probably the best summer flowering annual for massed displays, petunias also look wonderful in pots and hanging baskets. Available in a huge range of colors, some bicolored or striped, it can be planted in single colors or mixed colors—either way you will have a great display. Petunias grow to 10–16 in high, and they are reasonably fast growing.

CONDITIONS

Climate   Petunias love hot, dry weather and do not perform well in wet summers.
Aspect   Prefers full sun all day.
Soil   Must have very good drainage. Add compost or manure well ahead of planting time.

GROWING METHOD

Planting   In warm zones sow from early to middle spring, in cool zones not before the middle of spring. The very fine seed is hard to handle and should be barely covered. Plant out at 6–8 in intervals when 1–2 in high. Pinch out growing tips when 3–4 in high.

Watering   Water regularly to establish, and then allow soil to dry out between watering. Give a heavy soaking when needed.
Fertilizing   Don't overdo the fertilizer or you will have all leaves and few flowers. Complete plant food may be applied once or twice during the growing season but is not essential.
Problems   Rarely attacked by insects. Overwatering and poor drainage will cause yellowing and death of plants.

FLOWERING

Season   Throughout summer and into autumn if plants have been regularly dead-headed.
Cutting   Can be used as a cut flower but the main worth is in the colorful garden display.

AFTER FLOWERING

General   Cut back the whole plant after the first flush of flowers to encourage a second blooming. Once all flowering is finished or the plants are too straggly, dig them out.

PHLOX

Phlox drummondii

VARIETIES WITH POINTED PETALS are a charming variation on the usual rounded flowers. They look like so many stars.

MOST STRAINS of phlox come in mixed colors, mostly infinite variations on the theme of pink. Here are just a few in the range.

FEATURES

With their long flowering period, phlox are ideal for easy-care summer gardens. They grow 6–12 in high in a rounded, compact shape. The flowers have a wide color range—good strains include 'Bright Eyes' with a white eye and 'Twinkle' with star-shaped flowers. Suitable for massed planting or pots.

CONDITIONS

Climate Tolerates a very wide range of climates.
Aspect Needs full sun.
Soil Must have well-drained soil. Enrich soil with manure or compost to aid growth and improve moisture retention.

GROWING METHOD

Planting Sow in early spring in warm zones, not before late spring in cool zones. Sow seed directly into the ground or into pots and lightly cover it. Plant out at about 4 in intervals in the ground but in containers close plant for better effect. Pinch out growing tips when plants are 3–4 in high.

Watering Must be kept well watered, especially in very hot, windy weather, but soil should never become soggy.
Fertilizing Apply complete plant food monthly once plants are established.
Problems No particular problems.

FLOWERING

Season Throughout summer and into autumn in cool areas.
Cutting Not generally used as a cut flower but they last reasonably well if they are cut when flowers have just opened.

AFTER FLOWERING

General Cut back plants after first flowering as you may get a second flush. Remove them once they have finished flowering or if they are looking poor.

PINCUSHIONS
Scabiosa atropurpurea

JUST A FEW pink pincushions add spice to this mix. It also contains white candytuft and verbenas and pale pink gerberas.

PINCUSHIONS are at their best in a cottage garden mix. Here they grow with marguerites, forget-me-nots, irises and pale blue ixias.

FEATURES

Also known as mourning bride or sweet scabious, pincushions are lightly scented. The rounded heads of flowers come in shades of blue, mauve, purple, pink, white and crimson. With upright growth to 14–20 in and tall, wire-like stems, pincushions are attractive when used for massed planting and as filling between shrubs.

CONDITIONS

Climate Suitable for cool to tropical areas.
Aspect Prefers full sun and protection from wind.
Soil Prefers well-drained soil. Prepare soil by digging in organic matter well in advance, and give a light dressing of lime about a week before planting.

GROWING METHOD

Planting Sow in late winter–spring. Space out at 8–12 in when seedlings are 2–3 in high.
Watering Give deep, regular soakings in dry weather.
Fertilizing Give complete plant food about once a month when plants are well established.
Problems No particular problems.

FLOWERING

Season Summer and into autumn months if the flowers are cut regularly.
Cutting Excellent cut flower, which should last well with frequent water changes.

AFTER FLOWERING

General Dig out the plants when they have passed their flowering peak.

POLYANTHUS

Primula x polyantha

POLYANTHUS come in almost every color, but the wonderfully rich and pure blues are perhaps the most ardently sought after.

LOW-GROWING polyanthus make a carpet of jewel-bright colors. Except in the coolest areas they are happiest in light shade.

FEATURES

A cheerful little plant to brighten the dullest spot, polyanthus is perfect in pots or mass planted in the garden. Its very brightly colored flowers, on stems 6–8 in high, arise from neat clumps of bright green leaves. Perennial in cool climates, it is otherwise best treated as an annual.

CONDITIONS

Climate Can be grown in cool to tropical areas.

Aspect Needs semi-shade to shade in most areas but tolerates full sun in cool zones.

Soil Needs well-drained soil but with plenty of organic matter to help retain moisture, as the plants do not like to be bone dry at any time.

GROWING METHOD

Planting The very fine seed is difficult to sow and raise successfully. Sow on the surface of pots or trays and barely cover. Water from below. Sow in late summer as plants are slow to grow and flower. Plant out at 6–8 in intervals when large enough to handle. In cold areas pot them up into small pots and keep them under cover until spring.

Watering Keep soil just moist at all times, but never let it become soggy.

Fertilizing Once seedlings are 1–2 in high, apply complete plant food—use either soluble plant food biweekly or a granular plant food once a month.

Problems Slugs and snails find these plants very attractive and so can be a problem.

FLOWERING

Season Late winter to spring; later in cool areas. They flower over a long period if spent flowers are pinched off the plants regularly.

Cutting Not suitable as a cut flower. Potted plants may be brought inside and used as temporary indoor decoration.

AFTER FLOWERING

General Water plants until foliage dies down. In cool climates the plants can be lifted and divided while dormant. In warm, humid areas it is best to discard plants after flowering but if you keep them dry throughout the summer you will sometimes be able to get a second year's growth from them.

POOR MAN'S ORCHID

Schizanthus x wisetonensis

WHATEVER THEIR COLOR, these flowers display beautiful and elaborate markings of gold at their center.

THE RUFFLED FLOWERS do look a little like orchids, but Schizanthus wisetonensis is a cousin of the potato and tomato.

FEATURES

Also known as butterfly flower, poor man's orchid creates a stunning show when used for massed garden display, or when grown in large pots and hanging baskets. It grows to about 18 in high, with fern-like foliage and trumpet-shaped flowers in rich tones of pink, purple, magenta, pastels and white. The flower centers show contrasting color.

CONDITIONS

Climate   Suitable for cool or warm areas. Grown as conservatory plants in cold areas.

Aspect   Tolerates full sun to semi-shade but must have wind protection.

Soil   Must have well-drained soil, that has been enriched before planting with well-decayed manure or compost.

GROWING METHOD

Planting   Sow seed in autumn. In warm areas sow directly into the ground or into pots. In cool areas sow in pots and treat as conservatory plants. In the garden, space plants at 8 in intervals; in containers, plant closely. Pinch out growing tips when plants are 3–4 in high.

Watering   Keep plants well watered at all times, especially those in containers, but soil should never be soggy.

Fertilizing   Apply soluble liquid fertilizer monthly to promote good growth, continuing until the buds form.

Problems   No special problems.

FLOWERING

Season   In the garden flowers from late winter to the middle of spring. Conservatory displays in cool areas can usually be seen until early in the summer months.

Cutting   Not generally used as a cut flower.

AFTER FLOWERING

General   Discard plants once they have finished their flowering season.

POPPY

Papaver nudicaule

PETALS LIKE SILKEN CREPE provide the perfect setting for the symmetrical burst of stamens and stigmas at the center of the flowers.

POPPIES LOOK wonderful massed on their own, perhaps with just an edging to finish the bed. Here dusty miller sets off their warm tones.

FEATURES

Also known as Iceland poppy, this annual is a perennial favorite with young and old. The tall stems reach a height of 20 in, and finish with cupped flowers in a range of colors including red, yellow, orange, white and apricot. Often planted in parks and large gardens, it is equally suitable for massed planting in the home garden. Even six or seven plants will make a lovely show.

CONDITIONS

Climate Can be grown in cool and warm areas.
Aspect Needs full sun and wind protection.
Soil Needs well-drained soil. Add plenty of organic matter to soil well ahead of planting.

GROWING METHOD

Planting Sow seed in late summer or very early autumn in pots or trays. Barely cover the very fine seed. Plant out when seedlings are 1–2 in high, spacing them at about 8–12 in intervals. Take care not to break the fine roots when transplanting. Plant so that the crown of the plant is not too deep.

Watering Keep soil slightly moist at all times but never soggy, or the crowns will rot.
Fertilizing Apply complete plant food once plants are growing strongly in the ground. Repeat the application monthly.
Problems Overwatering or covering crowns of plants may induce gray mold. In dry springs they may be infected by spotted wilt virus. There is no cure for this problem.

FLOWERING

Season Late winter to spring. Don't allow tiny plants to flower. Remove any buds that form until the plant is well developed.
Cutting Excellent cut flower. Pick when buds are just opening for long vase life. Burn and scald stem ends before arranging.

AFTER FLOWERING

General Remove plants once flowering has finished or when flower quality is poor.

PORTULACA
Portulaca grandiflora

SINGLE-FLOWERED strains are available, but the double ones with their rose-like flowers are the most decorative and popular.

SATINY PETALS reflect the light. Portulacas come in just about every color but blue, always in bright, clear tones.

FEATURES

Portulaca, which is also known as sun plant, grows to only 6 in high. It has succulent leaves and brilliantly colored flowers that open only in the sun, although some modern hybrids remain open even on cloudy days. Portulaca is ideal for hot, dry spots in the garden, and for growing in containers and hanging baskets.

CONDITIONS

Climate Not suitable for very cold areas. Does well in tropical and warm zones.

Aspect Must have full sun all day; tolerates quite exposed, windy situations.

Soil Needs very well-drained soil, but otherwise it grows and flowers well, even where the soil is quite poor.

GROWING METHOD

Planting Sow seed from early spring to early summer. Sow seeds directly where they are to grow and thin them to about 4 in spacings once they are large enough to manage. Don't overwater the seedlings.

Watering Give regular watering until plants are established but then you can get by with an occasional heavy watering.

Fertilizing Performs well without any fertilizer, but if desired you can make an application of complete plant food once the seedlings are well established.

Problems No special problems but overwatering causes rotting and death of plants.

FLOWERING

Season Long flowering period through summer into the autumn months.

Cutting Unsuitable as a cut flower.

AFTER FLOWERING

General If conditions are suitable plants frequently self-seed. Remove plants once they begin to look straggly.

PRIMULA

Primula malacoides

THE WILD PRIMULA *is pale mauve; garden forms come in richer and brighter, but still cool, shades of pink and red.*

'GILHAM'S WHITE' *offers the most brilliantly pure white of any spring annual. It looks very fine here with yellow calceolarias.*

FEATURES

Very easy to grow, the primula has flowering stems that rise from neat clumps of bright green, slightly hairy leaves. Flowers are mauve, purple, cerise, pink or white. It reaches 12 in in height and is ideal for massed planting, as a filling between shrubs or for containers.

CONDITIONS

Climate   Can be grown in all cool and warm areas.
Aspect   Tolerates full sun in cool zones but prefers shade or semi-shade in warm zones.
Soil   Must have good drainage but does not tolerate dry soil. Adding some organic matter to the soil helps moisture retention.

GROWING METHOD

Planting   Sow in late summer in all zones; in warm zones sowing can extend into early autumn. Plant the very fine seed in trays or pots, barely covered. Plant out when 1–2 in high at 6–8 in spacings.

Watering   Keep soil just moist but never soggy throughout the growing season.
Fertilizing   Apply complete plant food once seedlings are well established. For best results continue this monthly until buds form.
Problems   Snails and slugs love primula seedlings, and so take precautions.

FLOWERING

Season   In warm zones from late winter until the middle of spring. Cool zone flowering is usually in summer.
Cutting   Although not used in the floral trade, flowers last a few days in a vase.

AFTER FLOWERING

General   Remove plants once they are past their best. They self-seed quite readily, but do not always come true and the following year's flowers may vary from those you planted.

RANUNCULUS

Ranunculus asiaticus

RANUNCULUS *are available in straight colors as well as mixtures.*
The best varieties are as full of petals as a camellia.

A MIXED BED *of ranunculus. The colors are bright and clear and*
blend harmoniously: the effect in the garden is warm and bright.

FEATURES

Ranunculus is also known as Persian
buttercup. Clear, bright colors are a
feature of this delightful plant, which has
many petalled flowers on straight stems
12–16 in high. The flowers are pink, white,
crimson, cerise, yellow and orange. Often
planted with anemones, ranunculus is
suitable for massed garden display and for
large containers.

CONDITIONS

Climate Can be grown in all cool to warm areas.
Aspect Needs an open, sunny position.
Soil Must have well-drained soil or tubers rot.
Mulching with compost or manure prevents
soil caking.

GROWING METHOD

Planting Sow seed in late summer in pots or where
they are to grow. Water in well but do not
water again until seedlings emerge, unless
weather is very dry. Plant the claw-like
tubers in autumn 1–2 in deep and 6 in
apart. Plant with claws down.

Watering Once plants are established, water heavily
about once a week. They may need
additional water in windy weather.
Fertilizing Soluble plant food may be applied biweekly
until buds appear but it is not essential.
Problems No special problems.

FLOWERING

Season Late winter to spring.
Cutting Excellent cut flower if the blooms are picked
when the flowers are fully formed but are
not wide open.

AFTER FLOWERING

General Once foliage has died down, the best tubers
can be lifted, dried (out of the sun) for a
couple of days, and then cleaned and stored
in an airy place. Second year flowerings may
not be as lovely as those of the first year but
are usually quite satisfactory.

ROSE MALLOW
Lavatera trimestris

THE NAME 'SILVER CUP' might suggest a white flower but in fact this prize-winning variety is clear, cool pink.

ROSE MALLOW looks best with lower plants in front. Here the large leaves of Bergenia cordifolia *provide an effective contrast.*

FEATURES

White, rose, pink and red flowers with a lovely sheen are the characteristic feature of rose mallow. The shrub-like plant grows from 32 in to over 3 ft tall and almost as wide. Use it to make a stunning display in the garden or grow single specimens in containers placed on patios or sunny corners.

CONDITIONS

Climate Can be grown in all warm to cool areas.
Aspect Prefers full sun.
Soil Needs good drainage but doesn't need very rich soil. Mulch around plants once they are growing strongly.

GROWING METHOD

Planting Sow in autumn in warm zones or spring in cool zones. Seed is easy to handle. Sow it where it is to grow.
Watering A heavy weekly soaking encourages deep roots that will sustain this tall plant through its growing season.

Fertilizing Apply complete plant food once the plants are established. The application should then be repeated monthly until such time as the buds first appear.
Problems No special problems.

FLOWERING

Season Spring in warm zones and summer in cool zones.
Cutting Suitable for cutting but the blooms are probably better appreciated when they are left in the garden.

AFTER FLOWERING

General If you want seed to plant next year, leave some flowers to age and dry on the plant. Otherwise, it is best to dig out the plants once they begin to look untidy.

SALVIA

Salvia splendens

ONCE CONFINED to scarlet, salvias are now available in a range of colors. The calyces make more of an impact than the short-lived petals.

AN EXCEPTION to the rule that bright flowers love the sun, the new salvia colors in fact hold best in light shade.

FEATURES

Also known as scarlet sage, these plants have upright growth with spikes of bright red flowers over a long period. Newer forms have striped, purple or white flowers. Most varieties of salvia grow about 10–12 in high but there are cultivars growing to 20 in. Salvia is used in massed garden displays but is also a useful plant for pots.

CONDITIONS

Climate   Suitable for any warm or tropical area. Can be grown in some cooler regions if given adequate protection from bad weather conditions. Not suitable for cold zones.

Aspect   Prefers a hot sunny spot.

Soil   Tolerates a wide soil range but drainage must be very good. Enrich very poor sandy soils with manure or compost ahead of planting.

GROWING METHOD

Planting   Sow in early spring in warm zones but wait until late spring in cool zones. Sow seed direct or in pots. Plant out when 1–2 in high.

Watering   Once plants are established, water heavily every week or so. They do not tolerate constantly wet soils.

Fertilizing   Apply liquid or granular fertilizer monthly to promote strong growth and good flowering.

Problems   Poor drainage and overwatering can cause plants to collapse.

FLOWERING

Season   Long flowering period throughout summer and autumn if plants are cut back after each flowering flush.

Cutting   Does not last well as a cut flower.

AFTER FLOWERING

General   In warm zones plants can be cut back hard and may flower again next season. Dig them out when they are no longer attractive.

HINT

Alternatives   Another species of salvia worth growing is *S. farinacea*, a short-lived perennial that is usually grown as an annual. It has velvety flowers in several colors, including a deep blue-purple shade.

SHIRLEY POPPY

Papaver rhoeas

THIS IS A CLASSIC Shirley poppy, its pink petals centered in white. They come in a wide range of delicate to rich shades of pink.

THE BLACK-CENTERED Flanders poppy, from which the Shirley poppies were developed in the 1880s by the vicar of Shirley in England.

FEATURES

Often used in meadow gardens, these poppies generally grow to about 20 in high but can be much taller in ideal conditions. The flowers are mostly red or pink but may sometimes be white. They come in single or double varieties. Shirley poppies are ideal for massed plantings but can also be used as accent plants.

CONDITIONS

Climate	Can be grown in cool and warm areas.
Aspect	Needs full sun with shelter from the strongest of winds.
Soil	Must have well-drained soil. Does best if compost or manure are added to the soil a few weeks before planting.

GROWING METHOD

Planting	Sow seed in later winter or very early spring. Barely cover the fine seed. Space out the seedlings in the garden at 12 in intervals once they are large enough to handle. Don't bury the plant crown.

Watering	Once plants are established, a heavy soaking once a week is best. In windy weather watering may need to be more frequent.
Fertilizing	Apply complete plant food three or four weeks after planting out and repeat monthly.
Problems	No special problems although there is a virus that causes yellowing and deformity of leaves. If this appears, immediately remove all the affected plants.

FLOWERING

Season	Late spring and summer.
Cutting	Suitable as a cut flower if stems are scalded before arranging.

AFTER FLOWERING

General	Remove plants once they are past their best.

SNAIL VINE

Vigna caracalla, syn. *Phaseolus caracalla*

THE FLOWERS are built on the same lines as sweet peas, but their curiously convoluted petals do make them look like snails.

THE SNAIL VINE never makes a solid sheet of color, but it is very decorative in both flower and leaf. Purple is the only color.

FEATURES

The curiously coiled light purple and cream flowers are a particular feature of this climbing plant and give it its common name. They are also scented. The plant grows to 9–15 ft in height. It is perennial in very warm areas, but it is best treated as an annual elsewhere as it dies down after flowering.

CONDITIONS

Climate   Grows vigorously in warm climates. Not suitable for cold areas.

Aspect   Prefers a position in full sun and one that is sheltered from wind.

Soil   Must have well-drained soil. Mulch with manure or compost once the plants are growing strongly.

Support   Requires chicken wire or trellis on which it can twine.

GROWING METHOD

Planting   Sow the seed in spring where it is to grow or in a pot. Don't sow too deeply—¾–1 in is about right. Water heavily after sowing but do not water again until the seedling emerges. If growing several vines, space them at least 12 in apart.

Watering   Give a deep weekly soaking unless weather conditions are extreme.

Fertilizing   Should not need much fertilizer. A dressing of complete plant food can be given when seedlings have established.

Problems   No special problems.

FLOWERING

Season   Summer and autumn.

Cutting   Not suitable for cutting.

AFTER FLOWERING

General   In cool areas the plant dies right down, and it is best removed and then replaced the following year.

SNAPDRAGON

Antirrhinum majus

OLD-FASHIONED snapdragons remain the favorites, although ones with double flowers and ones with wide open flowers are available.

ONE OF THE NEW dwarf strains, these are colourful for the front of a bed but lack the upright dignity of the taller types.

FEATURES

Snapdragons are best in massed garden displays but dwarf forms are suitable for pots and troughs. The dwarf forms grow to only about 10 in, while the tall varieties reach 24 in or more. The plants branch from the base and each branch ends in a spike covered with distinctive flowers. The lovely bright colors range from white and cream to yellow, orange, pink and red.

CONDITIONS

Climate   Suitable for warm to cool regions.
Aspect   Needs full sun with protection from the strongest wind.
Soil   Must have well-drained soil. Mulch the plants with compost or manure once they have become established.

GROWING METHOD

Planting   Sow at almost any time of year. Barely cover the very fine seed. When seedlings are large enough to handle, space them out in their permanent positions. Space dwarf forms at 6 in intervals, tall forms 12–16 in apart.

Watering   Needs regular heavy watering for long display but soil should never be soggy.
Fertilizing   Apply liquid or granular plant food once seedlings are well established. Repeat at monthly intervals.
Problems   Although there are some resistant varieties, snapdragons are very susceptible to rust, a fungal disease. Avoid overhead watering where possible and water early in the day. You may need to spray with a fungicide such as Maneb to control it.

FLOWERING

Season   Depends on when seeds were sown—they take 16–20 weeks from seed to flowering stage. Flowering is best from autumn to early spring.
Cutting   Very good cut flower. Scald the stems after picking.

AFTER FLOWERING

General   Cut plants back as you may get a second flowering flush. Discard plants once they are past their best.

SNOW-IN-SUMMER

Euphorbia marginata

THE FLOWERS of snow-in-summer are actually the little green affairs clustered at the center of each rosette of striped leaves.

GRAY-GREEN LEAVES and white bracts make a very long-lasting show and look cool and fresh even in a scorching summer.

FEATURES

Also known as snow-on-the-mountain, snow-in-summer is grown for its attractive foliage as the flowers are small and fairly insignificant. The green leaves are pointed and have an edging of white that can almost cover the topmost leaves. The plant grows to 3 ft and is best planted at the back of borders or in clumps. The milky sap is very poisonous.

CONDITIONS

Climate   Tolerates a very wide range of different climatic conditions.

Aspect   Prefers full sun but can manage with less. Needs some wind protection. Does not tolerate poor drainage.

Soil   Must have well-drained soil. Does not need rich soil but adding organic matter before planting helps growth.

GROWING METHOD

Planting   Sow seed during spring directly where plants are to grow.

Watering   Once plants are established, give a heavy watering once a week, but take care that you do not overwater.

Fertilizing   Grows well without supplementary fertilizer but if desired one application of complete plant food may be given when the seedlings are growing strongly.

Problems   No special problems but overwatering causes plants to rot.

FLOWERING

Season   Summer into autumn.

Cutting   Foliage may be used in arrangements but stems must be burnt or scalded to stop the milky sap bleeding.

AFTER FLOWERING

General   Remove plants by late autumn or early winter when they have started to fade. They will self-seed and you will usually find seedlings coming up the following year.

SPIDER FLOWER

Cleome hasslerana, syn. *C. spinosa*

NEW STRAINS of spider flower come in the mix of colors you see here, but the pale pink 'Rose Queen' remains the standby.

THE PLANTS look very permanent, and they are so strong and bushy they can stand in for shrubs while the shrubs are developing.

FEATURES

The spider-like flowers in pink, white or rose have narrow petals with long stamens. They appear over a long period, opening up down the length of the stem. Spider flowers are large annuals, growing to 5 ft high on a single stem, with lobed leaves. Plants are suitable for planting at the back of borders or they can be grouped as accent plants and sited throughout the garden.

CONDITIONS

Climate Tolerates a wide range of climates with the exception of very cold areas.

Aspect Prefers full sun with protection from very strong wind.

Soil Needs good drainage but tolerates a wide range of soils. The best results are from soils that have been improved by digging in manure or compost.

Support Although plants are so tall the stems are generally strong enough that they can grow without support.

GROWING METHOD

Planting Sow seeds directly where they are to grow in early spring (later in cool areas), spacing them at least 12 in apart, or sow them in groups that can be spaced out later by removing the weakest of the plants.

Watering Once plants are established, they tolerate fairly dry conditions but are best watered heavily about once a week.

Fertilizing Needs little supplementary fertilizer. Bone meal or complete plant food may be applied once seedlings are growing well, but it is not essential.

Problems No special problems.

FLOWERING

Season Long flowering period throughout summer and into autumn.

Cutting Not suitable as a cut flower.

AFTER FLOWERING

General Pull out plants once flowering is finished but do wear gloves as the stems are covered in small spines. Plants frequently self-seed and you should have some seedlings come up the following spring.

STATICE
Limonium sinuatum

STATICE FLOWERS are white and short lived: it is the beautifully colored calyces that make the striking display.

HANDSOME LEAVES as much as its purple flowers are the reason for growing Limonium latifolium, *a perennial form of statice.*

FEATURES

Statice is also known as sea lavender. It grows to about 16 in high with winged stems. Leaves are few and the small, ruffled papery flowers (calyces) come in a wide color range. Purple is most commonly seen but white, pink, apricot, yellow and blue can also be found. Use statice for general garden display but it is also ideal as a cut flower and as an integral part of dried flower arrangements. It is suitable for exposed coastal gardens.

CONDITIONS

Climate Can be grown in warm to cool areas.
Aspect Needs full sun all day for best results.
Soil Must have very well-drained soil but otherwise is not fussy about soil type.

GROWING METHOD

Planting Sow seed in late winter (early spring in cool areas) in pots or directly into the ground. Space out at 12–16 in intervals when seedlings are large enough to handle.
Watering Needs regular water to establish but once plants are established, allow soil to dry out between waterings. Don't overwater.

Fertilizing Complete plant food may be given once seedlings are established but this is not essential. They do not need regular feeding through the growing season.
Problems Poorly drained soils or overwatering kill plants quite quickly.

FLOWERING

Season Long flowering period throughout summer.
Cutting Ideal cut flower. Can be used for the vase or bunches can be cut and dried by hanging them upside down in an airy place. Dried flowers last a long time and retain their color well.

AFTER FLOWERING

General Dig out plants once all the flowers have been cut or faded.

HINT

Sea lavender The statice sold as sea lavender is usually the perennial *L. bellidifolium* or *L. latifolium*.

STOCK

Matthiola incana var. *annua*

A STUDY in family relationships: here a stock plant grows with its cousin the perennial wallflower, Cheiranthus mutabilis.

NOT ALL PLANTS will be double, even if you choose a double mix. Here there are a few "singles" mixed in, but they are still very pretty.

FEATURES

The sweetly scented flowers of stocks are borne in columns above the gray-green leaves. Many varieties are available, bearing single or double flowers in heights ranging from 12–32 in. There is a full range of pastel colors with some stronger purples, crimson and magenta as well. Stocks are lovely in massed plantings and the taller ones can be used as background plants in mixed borders.

CONDITIONS

Climate Not suitable for tropical gardens.
Aspect Needs full sun with wind protection.
Soil Must have well-drained soil. Incorporate manure or compost into the soil a few weeks ahead of planting and add lime about one week before planting.

GROWING METHOD

Planting In warm zones sow seed in late summer or early autumn, in cool zones in spring. Sow directly in the ground or in pots or trays, and cover lightly. When 1–2 in high place them into permanent positions 6–8 in apart.
Watering Give deep, regular waterings, probably once a week. Mulch around established plants to help conserve moisture.

Fertilizing Begin feeding once seedlings are about 4–5 in high. Use a complete plant food and repeat monthly until plants are in bud.
Problems Root rot may be a problem if plants are overwatered. They can also succumb to some of the fungal and viral diseases that affect cabbages as they are in the same family. Avoid planting stocks where these vegetables have been growing recently.

FLOWERING

Season Late winter and spring in warm zones, summer to autumn in cool zones.
Cutting Very good cut flower. Scald stems after picking and change vase water every couple of days.

AFTER FLOWERING

General In warm areas discard plants after flowering. In cool zones you can leave them in the ground where they may give a second blooming the following spring.

HINT

Doubles Even strains labeled "double" cannot be guaranteed to consist of all doubles, but about 75 per cent of these plants should be double.

STURT'S DESERT PEA

Swainsona formosa, syn. *Clianthus formosus*

FURRY GRAY-GREEN leaves point up the dazzling lacquer red and black of the clustered flowers of Sturt's desert pea.

IN NATURE Sturt's desert peas weave their way among low grasses, just as they do in this country garden.

FEATURES

These prostrate-growing plants have unusual pea-shaped red and black flowers on stems up to 12 in high. They are best grown in containers or well-raised garden beds, but some people have had success growing them in a vertically placed, terracotta drainage pipe. In ideal conditions plants may spread 3 ft wide. This is not easy to grow but it is a great talking point if grown successfully.

CONDITIONS

Climate   Ideally suited to dry areas. It is a challenge to grow this plant successfully in humid coastal regions.

Aspect   Must have full sun all day.

Soil   Must have very well-drained, coarse, sandy or gravelly soil.

GROWING METHOD

Planting   Difficult to transplant and so seed is best sown where it is to grow. Soak seed overnight in warm water or gently rub it between two sheets of sandpaper and then soak it for a few hours. Seed is best sown in autumn in warm areas and in late summer in cool ones.

Watering   Water regularly to establish plants but once they are established they should not need much watering at all. If there is no rain, water once every couple of weeks.

Fertilizing   Give weak soluble plant food every two or three weeks.

Problems   Plants dislike cold, wet conditions and high humidity. They rot very quickly if they are overwatered or if drainage of the soil is not very rapid.

FLOWERING

Season   Flowers at almost any time of year, depending on conditions. The main flowering period is late winter and spring, but in their desert habitat they can flower at other times after heavy rain.

Cutting   Unsuitable for cutting.

AFTER FLOWERING

General   Discard plants after flowering unless you live in an arid region.

SUMMER CYPRESS

Kochia scoparia

SOFTLY FUZZY foliage that turns russet in autumn is the main attraction here: the flowers are totally insignificant.

THE FIRM BUSHINESS of summer cypress here contrasts with the delicacy of summer flowers: tobacco flowers, salvias and godetias.

FEATURES

Summer cypress is a bushy annual that grows from 20 in to 3 ft high with soft, feathery foliage. The form *trichophylla*, the only one usually grown, has very fine foliage that is light, bright green in summer turning to a bronze red in autumn. The flowers are insignificant. It can be used as a filler, as a tall border around shrubs or as a background planting to other annual displays. In some areas it is a declared noxious weed: check before planting it.

CONDITIONS

Climate   Can be grown in cool or warm areas.
Aspect   Needs full sun to get the best foliage effects.
Soil   Needs well-drained soil but it need not be especially rich.

GROWING METHOD

Planting   Sow in containers, in warm zones in early spring, in cool zones in middle to late spring. Plant out when seedlings are about 2 in high, spaced out at 12–16 in intervals.

Watering   Once plants are established, a heavy watering once a week should be sufficient. In hot weather a mulch of rotted compost or manure over the root zone helps to conserve moisture.
Fertilizing Needs little fertilizer. Once seedlings are about 4–6 in high give a dressing of complete plant food.
Problems   No particular problems.

FLOWERING

Season   Flowers in late summer–early autumn. They are insignificant and of no decorative value.
Cutting Not suitable for cutting.

AFTER FLOWERING

General   Discard plants once they are past their best. They may self-seed.

SUNFLOWER

Helianthus annuus

THIS TRADITIONAL sunflower is golden, but you can also have fuzzy, all-gold doubles or singles in lovely shades of brown and gold.

A SUNFLOWER in full growth is a big, heavily leafed plant—most definitely to be planted at the back of the flower bed.

FEATURES

The sunflower is a delight for both children and adults. The tallest of the annuals, varieties reach 3–9 ft or so in height. Flowers have large dark centers with bright yellow petals; the foliage is somewhat rough to the touch. Sunflowers must be planted at the back of a bed or against a fence or wall. If space allows, plants can be massed.

CONDITIONS

Climate Can be grown in cool and warm regions.
Aspect Must have full sun and wind protection.
Soil Tolerates a wide range of soil conditions but needs good drainage. Soil enriched with manure or compost makes growth both rapid and vigorous.
Support Generally self-supporting if grown in a protected spot. Massed plants tend to support each other.

GROWING METHOD

Planting Sow in spring where they are to grow. Space seed at least 20 in apart—very tall varieties need wider spacings. Seeds are large and easy to handle.
Watering Once plants are established, water heavily about once a week.
Fertilizing Should not need supplementary fertilizer but an occasional liquid feed may make growth even faster.

Problems No special problems but watch out for snails. They may attack small plants but they also climb up mature plants to graze on the foliage and flowers.

FLOWERING

Season Throughout summer and autumn.
Cutting Very good cut flower but use a heavy-based vase or add some weight to the bottom of the vase to prevent it toppling over. Scald stems before arranging.

AFTER FLOWERING

General Dig out plants once they have finished flowering and start to look untidy.

HINT

Seeds If you wish to obtain seeds you must allow the flowers to remain on the plant until the petals have withered and browned and the central disc is quite dry and beginning to open out. Seeds can then be easily removed for dehusking and eating, or kept whole and saved for planting the following year. Edible sunflower seeds are gray with black or brown stripes, whereas those used for oil production are plain black.

SWEET ALYSSUM
Lobularia maritima

INDIVIDUAL FLOWERS *are small but they completely hide the leaves. They have a faint, pleasing scent of honey.*

'CARPET OF SNOW' *has here been used to make a Victorian-style patterned carpet with dark blue violas.*

FEATURES

Sweet alyssum is also known as sweet Alice. The main feature of this plant are the masses of tiny flowers in rounded heads. They are best known in white but pink, lavender and purple varieties are also available. Growing only 2–6 in high, sweet alyssum is ideal as an edging plant but it is also useful as a filler, or for planting in pots, troughs and baskets. Flowers are lightly scented.

CONDITIONS

Climate Suitable for growing in areas with cool or warm climates.
Aspect Prefers full sun but tolerates some shade.
Soil Must have well-drained soil but add organic matter only if soil is very poor.

GROWING METHOD

Planting Sow where plants are to grow or in pots. Lightly cover the fine seed. Space out at about 4 in intervals when plants are 1–2 in high. In warm zones best planting is in autumn or winter, but can be planted all year; in cool zones plant in the middle of spring.

Watering Give regular watering to establish but when growing strongly plants tolerate drying out.
Fertilizing Performs well without additional fertilizer but liquid or granular fertilizer may be applied monthly throughout the growing season.
Problems No special problems.

FLOWERING

Season Very long flowering period from about eight weeks after the seed is sown. Best flowering is usually in late winter throughout spring but they continue through summer and autumn with fresh sowings.
Cutting Not suitable as a cut flower. Shear the plants after the first flowering to induce a second flush.

AFTER FLOWERING

General When plants are sprawling and untidy, pull them out. Give them a good shake over the ground and you will find fresh seedlings emerging in a couple of months.

SWEET PEA

Lathyrus odoratus

BEAUTIFUL BLUE sweet pea flowers come from the smallest, most wrinkled seeds—never discard them just because they're wrinkled.

TALL-GROWING sweet peas need a trellis but they usually have the best scent. These look lovely against white woodwork.

FEATURES

Very sweetly perfumed flowers in a wide color range are the main feature of this climbing plant. The vine grows to 6–9 ft tall, with dwarf types reaching 8–20 in. Sweet peas are also suitable for baskets, tubs and spillover plantings. They grow best if planted in a different place each year.

CONDITIONS

Climate   Best in cool areas but grows well in warm ones. Not suitable for the tropics.

Aspect   Prefers full sun all day.

Soil   Needs well-drained soil. Apply lime, 3½ oz per square yard, before planting. Prepare beds ahead of time by digging in compost or rotted manure.

Support   Needs wire mesh for support as it grows as sweet pea is a tendril climber.

GROWING METHOD

Planting   Sow seed where it is to grow. Rows are best sited north–south. Seed may be soaked overnight to speed up germination but this is not essential. Plant seeds ¾–1 in deep and 3–4 in apart. In warm areas sow in middle and late autumn, in cool areas in spring.

Watering   Water thoroughly after planting but restrict watering until seeds germinate. Once seeds germinate, water them regularly to maintain good growth.

Fertilizing   Once plants are growing actively, apply weak liquid fertilizer weekly or bone meal or poultry manure monthly. Don't overfeed. If the leaf growth is too vigorous, you should stop fertilizing.

Problems   Overwatering or poor drainage can cause yellowing and death of plants. Powdery mildew can be a problem—it can be treated with sulfur.

FLOWERING

Season   In warm areas sweet peas flower from the middle of winter to the middle of spring. In cool areas they flower in summer.

Cutting   Excellent cut flower. Cut flowers when they are well formed—they should last a week with water changes. Frequent cutting prolongs the flowering period.

AFTER FLOWERING

General   If you want seed to plant next year, leave some flowers to set seed. Once plants are finished, dig them out or into the ground if the space is not needed for a following crop. Otherwise use the chopped up plant as mulch in another part of the garden.

SWEET WILLIAM

Dianthus barbatus

DWARF GROWING, the white-edged magenta flowers of 'Wee Willie' make a bright splash of color at the edge of this raised bed.

CLUSTERS OF SCENTED blooms held on long stems make these flowers ideal for cutting. They can have double flowers, too.

FEATURES

An attractive annual related to carnations and pinks, sweet William has flowers in pink, white, red, burgundy and bicolors. It has clumping growth to 12–14 in. Dwarf forms grow to 6–8 in. Sweet William makes an excellent bedding plant and it is very easy to care for.

CONDITIONS

Climate   Best in cool areas but grows well in warm zones. Not suitable for tropical areas.

Aspect   Needs full sun.

Soil   Needs well-drained soil that has been limed before planting.

GROWING METHOD

Planting   Sow the very fine seed in pots or trays for later transplanting. It is best sown in late summer or early autumn but can also be sown in spring. Sow seed in a good seed-starting mix, barely cover it and water carefully. Transplant the seedlings when they are 1–2 in high, spacing them 4–6 in apart.

Watering   Give regular deep watering but soil should never be soggy.

Fertilizing   Once plants are growing strongly, give them applications of liquid or granular complete plant food at monthly intervals.

Problems   No special pest or disease problems but poor drainage or overwatering kills plants.

FLOWERING

Season   Late winter throughout spring if spent blooms are regularly removed.

Cutting   Good cut flower, lasting quite well with regular water changes.

AFTER FLOWERING

General   Discard the plants when they have finished their flowering and when they no longer look very attractive.

HINT

Posy   Sweet William makes a lovely old-fashioned posy. It can be made into a posy on its own or you can add sprigs of forget-me-nots and white candytuft for a lighter effect.

TORENIA

Torenia fournieri

THE DARK MARKINGS *on the lower petals give torenias the name "wishbone flower." This is the original blue type.*

TORENIAS *are among the few summer annuals that grow equally well in sun or shade. They make compact, upright bushes.*

FEATURES

Torenia is also known as wishbone flower. Its pale violet flowers have deeper purple blotches on the lower petals and yellow inside. They can provide cooling color in the garden during hot summer weather. Torenia has compact growth to 8–12 in, which makes it ideal for massed plantings, or for use as a filler or in pots.

CONDITIONS

Climate   Dislikes cold conditions. Does well in cool to tropical areas.

Aspect   Needs full sun or semi-shade.

Soil   Needs well-drained soil. Dig in liberal amounts of manure or compost a few weeks ahead of planting.

GROWING METHOD

Planting   Sow the very small seeds in pots or trays in spring. Barely cover the seed with the seed-starting mix and take care not to dislodge them when watering. Space out the seedlings in the garden at 6–8 in intervals when they are large enough to handle.

Watering   Keep plants well watered, especially in hot, windy weather, but do not allow the soil to become waterlogged.

Fertilizing   Apply soluble plant food regularly to help maintain growth throughout the long flowering period.

Problems   No particular problems.

FLOWERING

Season   Throughout summer and autumn.

Cutting   Torenia is not generally considered as a cut flower, but it would look lovely if it were added to small arrangements.

AFTER FLOWERING

General   Pull or dig out the plants once flowering has stopped. They will sometimes self-seed, and they will then produce seedlings in the following year.

VERBENA

Verbena x *hybrida*

SOFT PEACH and apricot shades are a new development in verbenas. This one is the very attractive 'Romance Apricot.'

'PEACHES AND CREAM,' a fairly new variety, has quite subtle variations of tone in each cluster, as do many paler verbenas.

FEATURES

Valued for its long flowering period, verbena has clumping or prostrate growth 6–10 in high. It flowers in a range of mauve to purple shades, in white, pink or red. One newer variety has apricot flowers. Verbena is good for general garden display or for edging; it also does well in pots and baskets.

CONDITIONS

Climate   Grows well in cool and warm regions.
Aspect   Needs full sun for best results.
Soil   Must have well-drained soil. Does not need an especially rich soil.

GROWING METHOD

Planting   Sow seed in early spring where they are to grow or in pots. Plant out in the garden at 12 in spacings.
Watering   Give regular watering to establish but once established plants should be allowed to dry out somewhat between watering.

Fertilizing   Don't overfeed. One application of complete plant food can be given when plants are about 4 in high.
Problems   Overwatering or poor drainage kills plants. Some varieties are susceptible to powdery mildew—treat it with sulfur.

FLOWERING

Season   Long flowering period from late spring into the autumn months if the dead flowers are removed regularly.
Cutting   Not generally used as a cut flower but small pieces are attractive when added to a bunch of mixed flowers.

AFTER FLOWERING

General   Remove plants once they have finished flowering and are past their best.

VIOLA

Viola cornuta

MIXTURES OF TONING COLORS, here apricot and yellow, look especially good in containers. Shades of blue would be equally effective.

VIOLA FLOWERS can be a solid color or a blend of two shades (like those here), but they never display black blotches as pansies do.

FEATURES

Viola flowers are very like pansies but they lack the darker centers. They come in a clear, bright color range of yellow, apricot, blue, mauve, red and white, sometimes with two tones of the same color. Growing 6–8 in high in a mounded shape, they are suitable for massed plantings, but they are ideal for pots and containers, too.

CONDITIONS

Climate   Can be grown easily in both cool areas and warm areas.

Aspect   Prefers full sun but tolerates semi-shade.

Soil   Needs well-drained soil that has been enriched with manure or compost well ahead of planting time.

GROWING METHOD

Planting   In warm zones sow from late summer to late autumn; in cool zones it is best to sow in spring. Sow directly into the ground or into pots, and cover the seed lightly. Plant out in the garden at 6–8 in spacings when plants are 1–2 in high.

Watering   Once plants are established, water deeply about once a week, more frequently if weather turns hot and windy.

Fertilizing   Apply soluble liquid plant food biweekly once plants are well established.

Problems   No special problems but overwatering or poor drainage kills plants.

FLOWERING

Season   Late winter throughout spring in warm areas, summer in cool zones. Remove the spent blooms regularly or the plants will not continue flowering.

Cutting   Good cut flower. It can be used either in float bowls or in posies.

AFTER FLOWERING

General   Dig out once flowering has ceased or when plants have become lanky or straggly.

VIRGINIAN STOCK

Malcolmia maritima

FOUR-PETALED Virginian stock flowers are most common in mauve with a white eye but pink ones are also available.

A FAST GROWING but low plant covered in flowers, Virginian stock is ideal as an edging plant, beside a path or around a bed.

FEATURES

Virginian stock is ideal for stop-gap planting as plants can often grow from seed to flowering in four to five weeks. Plants grow 8–12 in high with small single, four petaled flowers in mauve, pink and white. They are excellent plants for borders, for filling gaps and for use in containers.

CONDITIONS

Climate   Can be grown in warm to cool areas.
Aspect   Prefers full sun but tolerates some shade.
Soil   Needs well-drained soil. If soil is very acid, apply a dressing of lime before planting.

GROWING METHOD

Planting   Sow where the plants are to grow as they don't transplant easily. Cover the seed lightly and water carefully so as not to dislodge it. Thin out the seedlings if too densely planted. Seed is generally sown in late winter and spring; it may also be sown at other times but not in high summer.

Watering   Give deep regular water once plants are growing strongly.
Fertilizing   Does quite well without supplementary fertilizer but soluble liquid fertilizer may be applied every couple of weeks.
Problems   No particular problems.

FLOWERING

Season   Spring is the main flowering season; Virginian stock generally flowers four to six weeks after it has been sown.
Cutting   Unsuitable as a cut flower.

AFTER FLOWERING

General   Once the floral display has finished, discard the plants.

WALLFLOWER
Cheiranthus cheiri

DOUBLE FLOWERED *wallflowers were Victorian favorites and are now available again. The blooms are long lasting.*

WHITE WALLFLOWERS *are not common but they can be found. This one opens a delicate and lovely shade of cream.*

FEATURES

Fragrant velvety flowers in a range of autumn tones—yellow, brown, cream, red and orange—characterize wallflowers, which are often planted for their distinctive sweet and peppery scent. Different varieties grow 12–20 in high. Plants are best used for garden display but may also be used in pots.

CONDITIONS

Climate	Grows well in cool to warm regions.
Aspect	Prefers full sun but tolerates part shade.
Soil	Must have very well-drained soil. Lime very acid soils before planting.

GROWING METHOD

Planting	Sow the seed directly where plants are to grow or into pots. Late summer or autumn sowings are best but in cold zones plants need protection over winter. Ideal plant spacing is 8–10 in apart.
Watering	Once plants are established, a deep weekly watering should be sufficient.

Fertilizing	Liquid or granular fertilizer may be applied once seedlings are growing strongly but it is not essential.
Problems	No special problems.

FLOWERING

Season	Late winter and spring. Frequent cutting prolongs the flowering period.
Cutting	Lovely cut flower that lasts well with frequent water changes.

AFTER FLOWERING

General	Remove plants once flowering stops.

HINT

Wall plant	These flowers really do grow in cracks in walls or stonework, and they are often seen in them, especially in England.

ZINNIA

Zinnia elegans

THIS IS 'OLD MEXICO,' *a daintier plant and flower than the usual zinnias. The flowers come in shades of mahogany and gold.*

ZINNIAS HAVE *the good habit of masking faded old flowers with new growth and bloom—hence the name "youth and old age."*

FEATURES

Zinnias are also known as youth and old age. The green zinnia, 'Envy,' is prized by flower arrangers, but zinnias come in a very wide color range, including purple, yellow, red, pink, cream and white. With an upright growing habit, they are best used in massed garden displays. Dwarf forms grow to 8 in high, normal varieties to 28 in or more.

CONDITIONS

Climate Grow only in warm or tropical areas.
Aspect Prefers full sun with protection from very strong wind.
Soil Must have well-drained soil. Tolerates a wide soil range but best in soils previously enriched with organic matter.

GROWING METHOD

Planting Best sown where they are to grow but they may be sown in pots. In tropical zones begin sowing in early spring; in warm zones in late spring. Space tall varieties 14 in apart, dwarf forms 8 in apart. Pinch out growing tips when plants are 4–6 in high.

Watering Deep weekly waterings are best once the plants are established.
Fertilizing In well-prepared soils plants should need little extra fertilizer but complete plant food may be applied at monthly intervals once the plants are growing well.
Problems Powdery mildew can be a problem—treat it with sulfur. Mites and aphids may also attack flowers. Snails need to be controlled, especially when plants are young.

FLOWERING

Season From late spring throughout summer.
Cutting Very good cut flower. Scald stems after picking and change vase water every couple of days.

AFTER FLOWERING

General Remove plants once flowering stops.

CUTTING FLOWERS

There is one point of view that annuals, like all flowers, look best in the garden, but we spend a lot of time indoors and we can often best enjoy our flowers there.

An arrangement of fresh flowers will brighten a room, bringing inside the beauties of nature that otherwise are left at the front door. Picking fresh flowers that you have planted and maintained over several months is one of the delights of gardening, but whether you are picking your own flowers or buying cut flowers, you will want to do all you can to get the best out of them and the longest vase life. These hints will help you achieve just that.

LEFT: *Harmony in contrast—huge yellow sunflowers and small blue cornflowers. Both will last five days or so in water.*

ABOVE: *The coneflower in close-up reveals its intricate structure.*

PICKING FLOWERS

When picking flowers from your garden, do so early in the morning or late in the afternoon. Cool them quickly by placing them in a bucket of cool water in a cool place and leave them to absorb water for an hour or so. This is especially important in hot summer weather. After this initial soaking you can then arrange them at your leisure.

BUYING CUT FLOWERS

If you are buying cut flowers, look for bright, fresh looking flowers that are just starting to open, and avoid flowers that have been standing in the sun or have been exposed to car exhaust fumes. Flowers with yellowing leaves on the stem or flowers with slimy stems have been in water for quite some time and are unlikely to be very satisfactory. When you get your flowers home, put them straight into a bucket of water without unwrapping them and leave them in a cool place to revive.

CLEAN VASES

Make sure your vases are perfectly clean. The stains in vases are usually bacteria that will get to work blocking the water uptake to the flower stems. Stains that are difficult to remove with normal cleaning may be removed by filling the vase with water and adding a few drops of household bleach. Leave this to soak for a couple of hours, rinse the vase well and refill with clean water.

CLEAN WATER AND PRESERVATIVES

Clean water is also most important for cut flowers. You can change the vase water daily or use a floral preservative —if you doubt that the effort or cost involved in using a preservative is worth while, test it for yourself by putting similar flowers in two separate vases. Add preservative to one vase and then leave the vases for a few days without changing the water. It won't be hard to tell the difference!

There are a number of very good preservatives on the market or you can make your own by combining 9 oz of lemonade (not diet type), 9 oz of water and half a teaspoon of household bleach. The sugar in the lemonade provides food for the flowers and the bleach kills off bacteria that would otherwise block the water-conducting tissues in the flower stem.

Check daily to see whether the water in the vase needs filling or changing. Some flowers with woody stems drink a lot of water, especially in the first two or three days after cutting, and so need the water refilled each day.

COLUMBINE
Columbines are useful cut flowers, both for their blooms and for the attractive gray-green foliage.

CANTERBURY BELL
Not a common cut flower, Canterbury bells may nonetheless be used to create an unusual effect.

ZINNIA
Zinnias are very good cut flowers, but be sure to change the water every few days. As soon as the flowers are cut the stems should be scalded.

ANEMONE
Anemones make excellent cut flowers if picked when the buds first open. Cut the stem cleanly with a sharp knife or sharp shears.

POPPY
Poppies make good cut flowers if picked when in bud. Plunge the ends of the stems into boiling water for about 20 seconds when first picked.

CONEFLOWER

The coneflower is a very good cut flower but be sure to pick them when the flowers are fully formed but before the petals have separated out too much.

STOCK

Stocks are excellent flowers for cutting. The stems should be scalded when first picked and be sure to change the water every few days.

VERBENA

Verbena is not commonly used as a cut flower but small pieces give an unusual look to any small mixed arrangement.

CALLIOPSIS

Pick calliopsis when the flowers are fully formed but the petals are still firm.

PANSY

Pansies are very successful as cut flowers, although their short stems mean they require special treatment. Include them in small posies or float them in a favorite shallow bowl.

COCKSCOMB

Cockscomb is not normally thought of as a cut flower but it can be used to add an unusual touch to an arrangement.

ARRANGING THE FLOWERS

Before arranging flowers in the vase, cut off a couple of inches of stem with sharp shears and be sure to remove any leaves that would be below the water level in the vase. Any left on the stem will rot quickly and pollute the water.

Daffodils, jonquils and tulips should not be placed with other flowers immediately after cutting as their secretions can cause other flowers to collapse prematurely. Place them in a separate vase for a few hours before adding them to a mixed arrangement.

If flowers develop bent necks, that generally means they have an air lock in the stem and so are unable to absorb water properly. Recut the stems under water and place them in cool, deep water for at least a couple of hours before attempting to re-arrange them.

Most flower stems absorb water best if cuts are made between nodes or joints; this is certainly true of carnations and hydrangeas. In the past many people believed that hydrangeas and some other flowers would absorb water better if the base of the stem was crushed with a hammer. This crushed tissue will in fact block up very quickly with bacteria and prevent the flower from drawing up water. Sharp, clean cuts are preferred as they allow the stem to absorb water most efficiently.

A number of annuals respond well to having the stems scalded for a few seconds. Place the end of the stem in boiling water for about 20 seconds but do keep the heads out of the steam or the blooms may be adversely affected.

MAKING THE MOST OF YOUR FLOWERS

Once the flowers are arranged in the vase, there are still a number of things you can do to make sure you get the best from them. For instance, cut flowers will not last well if you place the vase in full sun next to a window, or in rooms that are overheated. Strong drafts will also dry out cut flowers quite rapidly. And take care not to put vases of flowers next to your fruit bowl—the ripening fruit gives off ethylene, a natural ripening agent that ages flowers prematurely.

Be sure to remove individual flowers as they die. This will keep your arrangement looking attractive for much longer—mixed arrangements in particular can have their lives extended if the shorter lived flowers are removed.

Be aware, too, that some cut flowers, especially daisies and stocks, will produce an unpleasantly strong smell as they age in the flower vase.

FLOWERING CHART

PLANT COMMON NAME	SUITABLE CLIMATE	SPRING			SUMMER			AUTUMN			WINTER		
		EARLY	MID	LATE	EARLY	MID	LATE	EARLY	MID	LATE	EARLY	MID	LATE
Amaranthus	●○				●○	●○	●○	●○	●○				
Anemone	●○	○○	○○	○○	●								
Aster	●○				●○	●○	●○	●○					
Aurora daisy	○○		○○	○○	○○	○○	○○						
Baby blue eyes	○○	○○	○○	○○	○○	○	○						
Baby's breath	○○	○	○	○	○	○	○○	○○	○○	○○	○	○	○
Balsam	○○●	○○	○○	○○	○○●	○○●	○○●						
Begonia	○○	○○	○○	○○	○○	○○	○○	○○	○○	○○			
Bells of Ireland	○○●				○○●	○○●	○○●						
Black-eyed Susan	○○				○	○	○	○○	○○	○○			
Browallia	○○				○○	○○	○○						
Calendula	○○	○	○○	○		○	○	○					○
Californian poppy	○○		○○	○○	○○	○○	○○						
Calliopsis	○○●				○○●	○○●	○○●						
Candytuft	○○●	○○	○○	○○	○○●	○○●	○○●						
Canterbury bells	○○		○○	○○	○								
Cineraria	○○	○○											○○
Cockscomb	○○				○○	○○	○○	○○	○○	○○			
Coleus	○○				○	○	○	○○	○○				
Columbine	○○●		○	○○	○○●	○○●	○						
Coneflower	○○				○○	○○	○○	○○					
Corn cockle	○○			○○	○○								
Cornflower	○○			○	○	○	○						
Cosmos	○○					○	○○	○					
Dahlia	○○				○○	○○	○○	○○	○○	○○			
Delphinium	○○			○	○	○	○						
Dianthus	○○	○○	○○	○	○	○							○
Dusty miller	○○			○	○○								
English daisy	○○		○○	○○	○○	○	○						
Evening primrose	○○	○	○	○○	○○								
Everlasting daisy	○○			○○	○○	○○				○○	○○	○○	○○
Exhibition border	○○				○○	○○	○○						
Floss flower	○○◎	○○	○○	○	○○	○○	○○●	○					○
Forget-me-not	○○	○○	○○	○○									○○
Foxglove	○○	○	○	○	○○	○○	○○	○					
Globe amaranth	○○◎				○○●	○○●	○○●	○○●	○○	○○			
Godetia	○○		○○	○○	○								
Hollyhock	○○				○○	○	○○	○	○	○			
Honesty	○○		○○	○○	○○	○	○						
Johnny-jump-up	○○		○	○			○						
Kale	○○	○○	○○										○
Ladies' purses	○○	○	○										○
Larkspur	○○		○	○	○	○							
Linaria	○○	○	○		○	○							
Livingstone daisy	○○◎	○○	○○	○	○								○○

CLIMATE KEY	● HOT	○ TROPICAL	◐ WARM	◑ COOL	● COLD

PLANT COMMON NAME	SUITABLE CLIMATE	SPRING EARLY	SPRING MID	SPRING LATE	SUMMER EARLY	SUMMER MID	SUMMER LATE	AUTUMN EARLY	AUTUMN MID	AUTUMN LATE	WINTER EARLY	WINTER MID	WINTER LATE
Lobelia	◐◑	◐	◐	◐	◐◑	◐							◐
Love-in-a-mist	◐◑	◐	◐	◐	◐◑								
Lupin	◐◑	◐		◑									◐
Madagascar periwinkle	○◐		○	○	○◐	◐	◐						
Marigold	○◐◑			○	○◐	○◐	○◐	◐	○◐	○◐			
Meadowfoam	◐◑		◐◑	◐◑	◐◑								
Mexican sunflower	○◐				○◐	○◐	○◐						
Mignonette	◐◑	◐			◐	◐							◐
Monkey flower	◐◑		◐◑	◐◑	◐	◐							
Moon flower	○◐				○◐	○◐							
Nasturtium	○◐◑			○◐	○◐	○◐◑	◐						
Nemesia	◐◑	◐			◐	◐							◐
Painted tongue	◐◑				◐	◐◑	◐◑						
Pansy	◐◑	◐	◐	◐	◐	◐							◐
Paper daisy	◐◑	◐	◐	◐	◐◑	◐◑	◐◑						
Petunia	○◐◑				○◐◑	○◐◑	○◐◑	◐	◐				
Phlox	○◐◑				○◐	○◐◑	○◐◑	◐	◐				
Pincushions	○◐◑				○◐◑	○◐◑	○◐◑	◐	◐				
Polyanthus	○◐◑	○◐	○◐◑	◐◑	◐	◐							○◐
Poor man's orchid	◐◑	◐◑	◐◑	◐									◐
Poppy	◐◑	◐◑	◐◑										◐
Portulaca	○◐			○	○◐	○◐	○◐	◐					
Primula	◐◑	◐	◐	◑	◐	◐							◐
Ranunculus	◐◑	◐	◐◑	◐									◐
Rose mallow	◐◑		◐	◐	◐	◐							
Salvia	○◐◑				○◐	○◐◑	○◐◑	○◐	○◐				
Shirley poppy	◐◑			◑	◐◑	◐	◐						
Snail vine	○◐				○◐	○◐	○◐	○◐					
Snapdragon	◐◑	◐	◐			◐		◐					◐
Snow-in-summer	○◐◑				○◐	○◐◑	○◐◑						
Spider flower	○◐◑				○◐	○◐◑	○◐◑	○◐◑					
Statice	◐◑				◐◑	◐◑	◐◑						
Stock	◐◑	◐	◐	◐		◐	◐	◐					◐
Sturt's desert pea	◐◑	◐◑	◐◑	◐									◐
Summer cypress	◐◑						◐	◐					
Sunflower	◐◑				◐	◐◑	◐◑	◐◑	◐◑				
Sweet alyssum	◐◑		◐	◐	◐◑	◐◑	◐◑						◐
Sweet pea	◐◑	◐	◐			◐	◐				◐	◐	
Sweet William	◐◑	◐◑	◐◑	◐◑									
Torenia	○◐◑				○	○◐◑	○◐◑	○◐	○◐				
Verbena	◐◑			◐	◐	◐◑	◐◑	◐	◐				
Viola	◐◑	◐	◐	◐	◐	◐	◐						◐
Virginian stock	◐◑	◐	◐◑	◐◑	◐	◐							
Wallflower	◐◑	◐◑	◐◑	◐									◐
Zinnia	○◐			◐	◐○	○◐	○◐						

INDEX

Page numbers in *italics* refer to illustrations

K

kale, 52, 106
Kochia scoparia, 91

L

ladies' purses, 53, 106
larkspur, 10, 54, 106
Lathyrus odoratus, 94
Lavatera trimestris, 81
Limnanthes douglasii, 62
Limonium bellidifolium, 88
L. latifolium, 88
L. sinuatum, 88
linaria, 55, 106
Linaria genistifolia, 55
L. maroccana, 55
L. purpurea, 55
Livingstone daisy
    see daisy, Livingstone
lobelia, 10, 57, 107
Lobelia erinus, 57
Lobularia maritima, 93
love-in-a-mist, 10, 58, *68*, 107
love-lies-bleeding, 12
Lunaria annua, 50
lupin, *9*, 59, 107
Lupinus hartwegii, 59
L. luteus, 59
L. texensis, 59

M

Madagascar periwinkle, 60, 107
Malcolmia maritima, 99
marguerite, *41*, 74
marigold, 10, 61, 107
    African, 61
    English, 23
    French, 61
    pot, 23
Matthiola incana var. *annua*, 89
meadowfoam, *16*, 62, 107
Mexican sunflower
    see sunflower, Mexican
mignonette, 64, 107
Mimulus species, 65
molucca balm, 20
Molucella laevis, 20
money plant, 51
monkey flower, 10, 65, 107

moon flower, 66, 107
mourning bride, 74
Myosotis sylvatica, 45

N

nasturtium, 6, 7, *57*, 67, 107
nemesia, 68, 107
Nemesia strumosa, 68
Nemophila menziesii, 16
Nigella damascena, 58

O

Oenothera biennis, 41
O. rosea, 41
orchid, poor man's, 10, 76, 107
ornamental cabbage *see* kale

P

painted leaves, 30
painted tongue, 69, 107
pansy, 70, 98, *105*, 107
Papaver nudicaule, 77
P. rhoeas, 83
paper daisy *see* daisy, paper
penstemon, *9*
pests, 7
petunia, *3*, 10, 11, *43*, 72, 107
Petunia hybrida, 72
Phaseolus caracalla see Vigna caracalla
phlox, 73, 107
Phlox drummondii, 73
pincushions, 74, 107
poached egg flower, 62
polyanthus, 10, 11, 75, 107
poor man's orchid, 10, 76, 107
poppy, *6*, *46*, *68*, 77, *104*, 107
    Californian, 24, 106
    Flanders, *83*
    Iceland, 77
    Shirley, 83, 107
portulaca, *6*, 10, 78, 107
Portulaca grandiflora, 78
primula, 5, 6, 10, 11, 79, 107
Primula malacoides, 79
P. obconica, 45
P. x *polyantha*, 75
Prince of Wales feathers, 29
prince's feather, 12

R

ranunculus, 10, 11, 80, 107
Ranunculus asiaticus, 80
Reseda odorata, 64
rocky mountain garland, 48
rose mallow, 8, *46*, 81, 107
Rudbeckia, 5
R. hirta, 21

S

Salpiglossis sinuata, 69
salvia, *9*, 10, 63, 82, *91*, 107
Salvia farinacea, 82
S. splendens, 82
Scabiosa atropurpurea, 74
scarlet sage, 82
Schizanthus x *wisetonensis*, 76
sea lavender, 88
seed, 6
    saving, 7
    sowing, 6
seedlings, 6
Senecio cineraria, 39
S. x *hybridus*, 28
Shirley poppy *see* poppy, Shirley
slipper flower, 53
snail vine, 84, 107
snapdragon, *3*, 7, *55*, 85, 107
    baby, *55*
snow-in-summer, 86, 107
snow-on-the-mountain, 86
soil preparation, 6
Solenostemon scutellarioides, 30
spider flower, 11, 87, 107
starflower, 71
statice, 88, 107
stock, *68*, 89, *105*, 107
    column, 11
    Virginian, 99, 107
Streptosolen jamesonii, 22
Sturt's desert pea, 90, 107
summer cypress *see* cypress, summer
sun plant, 78
suncups, 41
sunflower, 6, 92, *103*, 107
    Mexican, 63, 107
Swainsona formosa, 90
sweet Alice, 93
sweet alyssum, *5*, 10, 11, 93, 107
sweet pea, 6, *84*, 94, 107
sweet rocket, 54
sweet scabious, 74
sweet William, 95, 107

T

Tagetes, 61
T. erecta, 61
T. patula, 61
Texas bluebonnet, 59
Tithonia rotundifolia, 63
tobacco flower, *91*
torenia, 10, 96, 107
Torenia fournieri, 96
toad flax, 55
Tropaeolum majus, 67
tulip, 105

V

vases, 104
verbena, 10, 74, 97, *105*, 107
Verbena x *hybrida*, 97
Vigna caracalla, 84
viola, *5*, 10, 11, *40*, 93, 98, 107,
Viola cornuta, 98
V. tricolor, 51
V. x *wittrockiana*, 70
violet
    bush, 22
    native, 36
Virginian stock *see* stock, Virginian

W

wallflower, 10, 89, 100, 107
watering, 7
wishbone flower, 96

Y

youth and old age, 101

Z

zinnia, 10, *11*, 101, *104*, 107
    dwarf, *3*, 101
Zinnia elegans, 101

This 1997 Crescent edition is published by Random House Value Publishing, Inc.,
201 East 50th Street, New York, N.Y. 10022
http://www.randomhouse.com/

Random House
New York • Toronto • London • Sydney • Auckland

Originally published by Murdoch Books®, a division of Murdoch Magazines Pty Ltd,
213 Miller Street, North Sydney NSW 2060 Australia

Managing Editor, Craft & Gardening: Christine Eslick
Designer: Jackie Richards
Photographs: Lorna Rose (all unless specified otherwise);
Denise Greig (p. 13L); Gregory Lewis (pp. 30R, 69L and R, 76L)
Stirling Macoboy (pp. 16L, 17, 22, 47R, 48R, 55, 91L and R); Tony Rodd (p. 54L and R)
Illustrator: Sonya Naumov
CEO & Publisher: Anne Wilson
International Sales Director: Mark Newman

Printed and bound in the United States of America

A CIP catalog for this book is available from the Library of Congress
ISBN 0-517-18404-4
87654321

Front cover: Petunias 'Dreams' in salmon and sky blue
Back cover: Pansy (top left), coleus (top center), Madagascar periwinkle (top right), cosmos (bottom left), begonia 'Fair Lady' (bottom center), zinnia (bottom right)
Inside back cover: Yellow sunflowers and blue cornflowers
Title page: Sweet pea